Concepts and Choices

FOR TEACHING

Meeting the Challenges in Higher Education

William M. Timpson and Paul Bendel-Simso

Magna Publications, Inc.
Madison, Wisconsin

2718 Dryden Drive
Madison, WI 53704

Printed in the United States of America
01 00 99 98 97 96 8 7 6 5 4 3 2 1

Cover design by Tamara L. Cook

Library of Congress Cataloging-in-Publication Data

Timpson, William M.
Concepts and choices for teaching: meeting the challenges in higher education/William M. Timpson, Paul Bendel-Simso.
p. cm.
Includes bibliographical references (p.).
ISBN 0-912150-40-08
1. College teaching. 2. Effective teaching. 3. Learning.
I. Bendel-Simso, Paul, 1963- II. Title.
LB2331.T48 1996
378.1'25--dc20 96-32719
CIP

DEDICATION

To Kellee and her teachers.
May your shared journey be rich and rewarding. (BT)

Table of Contents

FOREWORD

The challenge to "teach well" is an enormous one, and as a teacher you face it every day of your professional life. Indeed, the life of higher education is dependent upon the ability of teachers to perform their role well, but the nature of this role — and of the expectations placed upon you — can be confusing. Just what is your responsibility to your students? Are you an authority figure, or can you also be their friend? Out of twenty-four hours in a day, how many of them should you devote to your students? Can you treat the class as a group, or do you need to attend to each student individually?

Even if you are able to answer these questions to your own satisfaction, even more fundamental questions arise: What are you teaching? A particular subject? A general methodology? Should you be teaching your students how to learn, or is that even any of your business? Should you worry about their motivation, about what interests them, or is success in higher education purely a matter of student initiative?

The title of this book suggests an approach to some of these issues. In the following pages, you will find an overview of many of the concepts that researchers from a range of disciplines use to make sense of what we do when we work with students: we reference scholars in education and psychology primarily — particularly those who specialize in teaching and learning. But we also include experts in human development, social, experimental and counseling psychology, higher education, and the related social sciences, as well as "regular" professors who are interested in teaching and learning generally. These different ideas about education — these concepts — provide us with choices that need to be confronted if we are to improve and succeed as instructors.

It is our conviction that bringing these concepts and choices to your attention will help you take control of the process of becoming the best teacher possible. We also believe that it will enhance your confidence in teaching, your success in facilitating student learning, and your enjoyment of your students as individuals. Whether you are new to teaching or quite experienced, we know that your teaching will be more effective and efficient once you become aware of the conceptual framework around which your personal teaching style is built.

Concepts and Choices is not intended to be a handbook or an instructional manual; it is an offering of the best of what is available in the realm of teaching and learning, both theoretical and practical, current and historical. Far from presenting a single prescription or paradigm, what you'll find in these pages is a diverse collection of ideas and strategies which have proven useful over time and in various settings. As the reader, your job is to choose from among these options, and in making your choices, discover ways in which your teaching style must be tailor-made to your needs and gifts as an individual.

The main belief running throughout the book is that any debate about whether good teaching is inborn or learned would be a futile one. Some people are perhaps naturally better with students than others, but it is obvious that teachers, at any level, can improve their performance if they are willing to study what they're doing, reflect upon why they're doing it, and take steps to change what they're doing if necessary. Effective teaching involves an identifiable set of skills, and these skills can be learned and developed. For this to happen, however, you must approach your craft deliberately, with the understanding that the choices you make will shape your performance as a teacher and your students' success as learners.

Science and Art

Another way to interpret the title of this book is to say that successful teaching not only demands your commitment to the gaining of certain skills, it also requires you to infuse these skills with your own personal style. The science of instruction is the full range of options, the underlying theories and the practical strategies, which you can employ to enhance your presentations and facilitate learning. In addition, the science of instruction takes into consideration differences among your students: their background, preparation, motivation, and needs, as well as their individual learning styles. We take up the issue of student diversity throughout this book, knowing that your students will experience greater success once you have broadened and deepened your own understanding of instruction, and once your students understand the role they are to play in the classroom.

On the other side of the equation lies the art of instruction, where your own gifts and abilities come into play — your strengths, experiences, training and intuition, your intelligence, values and personality, your creativity. Much like actors who begin with a thorough understanding of the script and their craft — the science or knowledge of performing, if you will — but then add their artistry to breathe life and believability into the lines, teachers must breathe life into their "scripts." Remember that no one pays to see a play read. We go for the magic of the human interpretation, and the same may be said of the classroom.

Artistry is that unique mixture of energy and focus which defines you. Artistry is also your ability to make those countless decisions as your lesson unfolds — when to continue, when to rephrase or stop and probe, when to observe, to listen, what to say in response to a question or comment, when to step in or let events evolve as they will, what props to use, issues of timing and pacing, when to shift gears or try something wild, how to assess mood or deal with pauses and silence.

With experience, you gradually find the mixture that is right for you, your discipline, and your students. Admittedly, much in this mixture is ever-chang ing, varying with the chemistry of each course and each set of students, and evolving over the years as your experience grows. One of the challenges we all face as instructors is how to keep our teaching fresh and vital, so that we can be open to the creative possibilities in every course and with each group of students. In the beginning, these demands might seem a drain on your (often too finite) energies. In the long run, however, this sensitivity to the ongoing interplay of multiple variables — to subtleties, rhythms, personalities, and differences — and this concern for artistry and intuition can become a source of regular revitalization for you.

Ultimately, your abilities to combine science and art — theoretical concept and practical choice — will not only make you more natural and comfortable as a teacher, it will help you to connect more closely with your students, which is, after all, the fundamental objective of instruction. Creating this space of learning, where you can effectively relate to your students and where the students can relate to one another means creating an environment in which everyone feels challenged to learn and to think, and where students can challenge themselves to grow intellectually.

Education no longer happens in an ivory tower or in a social vacuum (if it ever did), nor is it free of real complications or difficulties. At present, the complexities of postsecondary teaching seem to be growing as fast as the knowledge base we are all expected to impart, and the future will surely demand more, not less, from instructors. As higher education worldwide continues to attract more and more students, the increasing diversity of students brings ever new challenges. How do we teach students this expanding knowledge-base and evolving skill-base when backgrounds, academic preparation, and motivation are very different? How can we create learning environments which will accommodate those students just out of high school as well as all those returning to school later in life? How do we address the needs of part-time students who are raising children or working while they attend school? How do we adapt to students with special needs? The answers to these questions, and many others, are not matters solely for administrators, nor do they fall outside the realm of the teacher's interests. In fact, these nuts-and-bolts issues are fundamental to the health of our profession, and our intelligent response to them is vital to our continued prosperity.

Throughout this book, we emphasize our conviction that the best teaching is teacher-directed and student-centered — sensitive to student questions and confusion while it actively mobilizes student energies and challenges them to think critically and creatively. And even as you employ the latest in technology and equipment, the best teaching can be quite succinctly described as *effective communication*. Conveying information, creating an efficient classroom environment, establishing teacher/student rapport, and all the other elements that make for effective teaching can be regarded as aspects of a general goal: to connect in teacher and learner, and to give both a genuine sense of responsibility, of "ownership" of the classroom. When this end is accomplished — no matter how, or with what tools — your career should be more fulfilling, and your students should gain from what you have to offer them.

The Design of the Book

The contents are arranged into two parts. Part I gives a broad, informal overview of the theoretical underpinnings of teaching and learning in higher education from a variety of perspectives — educational, psychological, developmental, social, and more. Here we also discuss the nature of the modern class and student. In Part II, we present a collection of different practical teaching formats and models, from lecture to discussion, from process-driven to outcome-driven teaching, and from student work-groups to individualized computer lessons.

It is our hope that this design will help you connect your own experiences as a student and a teacher with the range of options available for improving instruction, hopefully stimulating a fresh consideration of those issues which affect learning within and across the various academic disciplines. Finally, we have also designed this book to be an accessible and effective reference for self-examination of your own teaching style: explanations are relatively brief and references are limited primarily to those which we consider important in a historical context; numerous examples punctuate each chapter; and exercises offer ideas for further self-study.

Acknowledgments

First and foremost, I want to thank all those colleagues who let me into their classes to watch them teach and listen in to student conversations about learning. I know that my understanding of the instructional process as well as my own abilities as a teacher have grown immeasurably. Many of these teachers are named throughout the text.

In addition, I want to credit all those who have aided me in a variety of ways but whose names do not appear. To Barb Nelson, my colleague and friend for many years, a caring and energetic teacher of teachers with whom I have worked closely for many years. To colleagues at the University of California, Santa Cruz, who supported my efforts to bring back to life a campus commitment to innovative and high-quality undergraduate education: in particular, to John Isbister and Leo Laporte. Likewise, to colleagues at the University of Queensland in Brisbane, Australia, who joined with me to find better balance to the pressures on faculty to produce research: in particular, to Andrew Lister, Linda Rosenman, and Ian Reinecke.

I also have to thank all those students in my own classes who have appreciated my efforts at innovation and improvement, and then given their feedback honestly.

Looking back I must give credit to all of my teachers who inspired me with their commitment to quality, inspiration and my own learning.

Finally, I want to thank those who helped with earlier drafts of this manuscript: in particular, to Eileen Tanner. And finally, I need to thank those at Magna Publications who supported our work on this manuscript, most importantly, Linda Babler.

Bill Timpson

The effort I put into this book has been greatly supported by my wife, Dr. Mary Bendel-Simso. Throughout the time I have been involved in this project, she has frequently taken on the roles of consultant, writing coach, and grammar police. In addition, a lot of what I know about successful teaching on the college level comes from her courses on composition and American literature. She is doubly to be thanked in that she was conscripted for these roles by virtue of being present in the room when I was writing.

I would also like to extend my gratitude to Linda Babler at Magna Publications for her patience and skill in keeping *Concepts and Choices* on track through its numerous metamorphoses over the past months.

Paul Bendel-Simso

PART I

Theoretical Overview of Teaching and Learning

CHAPTER ONE

The Climate for Learning

The classroom is a varied, exciting, even mysterious place, a place where happenings change by the day, the hour, the mood of the individuals who gather there.

Kenneth Eble
The Craft of Teaching

The most important tool that you have at your disposal as a teacher is the space in which you do your job. Here we are not simply referring to the classroom space with its chairs and desks where you do your thing every few days, but to the environment which you as a teacher create, and into which you project yourself and your personality. The classroom is, as much as anything else, a communicative and social space where student ambitions and teacher expectations meet, and it is your obligation as a teacher to make this meeting a fruitful one. It doesn't matter if your class meets in a modern lecture hall equipped with television and desk-side computer terminals, or in the dankest, windowless sub-basement, your responsibility as the instructor is to take that space — wherever you meet students — and turn it into a dynamic site for learning.

In other words, you must be both manager and creator of *climate* — a steward of the attitudes and feelings, joys and anxieties, the sense of accomplishment, etc., which students and instructors share during class, with an eye toward making the time spent challenging and profitable. (The word "profit" is telling, since this use of the term *climate* originated in industry as management focused on the morale of employees with the goal of enhancing productivity.) Climate has begun to receive more attention as

> Over the years, physicist Sandy Kern has managed to balance his interest in teaching and learning with an active research agenda which has included regular working visits to Argonne National Labs. Knowing full well the kinds of creative energy needed for explorations at the forefront of his discipline, Kern often ventures away from prepared notes to challenge student misconceptions and push for deeper understanding. Along the way he watches intently for signs of confusion, frequently polling to see how many students agree with this or that conclusion. Because many students are understandably anxious, and some terrified, about admitting their confusions in a class of three hundred, Kern will go to some length to make the climate safer. Early in one semester, for example, he stopped after working a problem and said to his class, "Look, there is no such thing as a foolish question, only a foolish answer, so I'm the only one at risk here."

instructors at all levels attempt to meet new and different challenges in promoting learning.

A clue to the direction of this shift in attention can be found in one of its sources — the students: it isn't possible to teach in higher education today and not encounter students who want more say in the decisions that affect them. They not only want lessons to be directly relevant to their lives, they want to be involved more closely in the planning and conduct of their own education: their teachers need to respond accordingly. More and more, active two-way participation in the learning process is becoming the standard by which effectiveness in teaching is measured, and if you make a conscious effort to provide for a lively and engaging climate, you will find yourself both liking your job more, and doing it better.

The underpinnings of the notion of classroom climate reach back about twenty years. In the seventies, CFK Limited, a Denver-based philanthropic foundation dedicated to improving the learning environment of schools, supported the publication of a series of monographs detailing what "educational climate" means and how schools can improve by paying attention to it. In one of these publications, Shaheen and Pedrick (1974) define climate in terms of student and teacher productivity and satisfaction. For them, *productivity* includes:

- Achieving basic skills
- Developing constructive attitudes
- Developing and expanding an adequate knowledge base
- Clarifying values and purposes
- Utilizing inquiry and problem-solving processes

Satisfaction means:

- Gaining a sense of personal worth
- Enjoying school as a pleasant place to live and work
- Gaining rewards from participation in worthwhile activities

Fox and his group (1974) outline several general factors that characterize a positive educational climate, including respect, trust, high morale, opportunities for input, continuous professional growth, cohesiveness, renewal, caring, commitment to goals, and ease of communication. In 1980, Lezotte and his colleagues focused almost exclusively on productivity in their definition of educational climate as "the norms, beliefs, and attitudes ... that enhance or impede student achievement." These researchers discovered a continuous interplay between students' morale and their performance — an interplay which both research and intuition suggest must be in place for effective learning to take place. Central to this equation, however, is your role: as the teacher, you are responsible for this climate, and your role within it is that of monitor and director.

If you look for it, you can see a great deal of support for this increased concern for morale, feelings, and attitudes.

Biologist Todd Newberry points out that there are more disabled students on campus than many realize, particularly if one takes into consideration those whose disabilities are invisible. Conditions as varying as learning disabilities, diabetes, heart conditions, and auditory or visual impairments can all fall into this category; and all of these problems can have a profound effect upon a student's academic success. Before writing off the "stupid," "demanding," or "needy" students, and giving up on them too soon, make sure you have considered the possibility that these students may be suffering from a real handicap and do not themselves acknowledge its existence. Help can be found for almost all of these students, and the first line of defense (and often their last) is the teacher. In addition, be sensitive to curricular disabilities resulting from poor academic preparation or advising; or employment disabilities stemming from excessive interference of work; or temporary psychological disabilities caused by any number of problems, including those stemming from relationship conflicts or from a death of a family member or friend.

Newberry uses a variety of methods to make his class disabled-friendly. Whenever possible, for example, he schedules his large lecture classes at the day's earliest hour, so he can open the doors as much as ninety minutes early for exams to accommodate those who need additional time, without interfering with a class before his. He also asks students to identify any disabilities that they may have at the beginning of a course so that he can consider how to accommodate them throughout the quarter. Nothing succeeds like your personal vigilance, however, and keeping an eye on struggling students and seeking feedback on a regular basis can often tell you how to best help them cope with the demands placed upon them.

Cori Mantle-Bromley teaches a graduate education class on multicultural and special populations. Because course content deals with so many sensitive issues, Mantle-Bromley really needs active and informed participation if students are to find a constructive path through all the potential "landmines." Without careful attention to the assigned readings, discussions can quickly spin off into heated exchanges which are fueled by both popular media and prevailing prejudices. Accordingly, she will thank her students for coming to class prepared to refer to the assigned readings. Instead of just leaving it as a requirement or expectation, she will pay close attention to the level of student preparation, and how it affects the discussions in class. You can certainly find much support for what Mantle-Bromley does among behaviorists who constantly chide teachers for concentrating too much on the consequences of failure rather than upon the rewards of success.

The answer to the question "What is a good learning climate?" is somewhat elusive. There are certain common tendencies among all healthy classroom environments. For instance, a teacher's own engaging personality can frequently bring out the best in individuals and groups. Psychology professor Elliot Aronson teaches an introductory course on social psychology to large classes. Because he has an international reputation and has written one of the leading college textbooks in the field, students could feel intimidated in the class. The climate, however, is open and friendly, and students participate easily. Aronson mixes his own natural friendliness with a relaxed pace to create a positive rapport, which students clearly value.

For example, to improve learning on campus, Lowman (1984, 16) places a heavy emphasis on climate without using the word expressly, encouraging instructors to focus on intellectual excitement and interpersonal rapport, nurturing students' academic drive as well as their emotional well-being. In his view, the best teachers combine their academic orientation with an open, fair, highly student-centered approach to instruction.

Central to a positive climate is the responsibility that both teachers and students share for the success of any particular class. Teachers in higher education need to come prepared and energized for class, yet they must also be flexible, and sensitive to student needs. This means that you need to know how you can be best prepared, both physically and intellectually. If you don't know how you are best prepared, then experiment: a period of meditation, a last-second review of notes, lecturing to yourself in your office before class — try everything, and eventually some things will click. In addition, we can remind students that they too must come prepared and willing to put forth the effort required to maximize their success. This includes not only mastering the required material, but also expressing their needs and concerns in a constructive, timely, and reasonable manner.

How can you improve your classroom climate? In the following pages we have gathered a number of suggestions; as you will see, many come from colleagues who have shared what works for them to encourage a free and inclusive interchange of ideas, information, experiences, and reactions, and ensure that a diverse student body can be transformed into a cohesive learning community.

A Humane Environment

Teachers can improve the climate for learning in any number of ways. Initially, you can start by promoting a sense of empowerment on the part of students by involving them as much as possible in decisions which affect them and their learning. Any way in which their energy and talents are brought into more constructive use can be a strategy to improve the climate, and the results can often be seen immediately: instead of sitting through class for an hour, and then later complaining among themselves — and all too frequently, these complaints are well-founded — students can be challenged during class to convert their dissatisfactions into a force for positive change. Instead of feeling that they must simply either endure the status quo or rebel, they can be asked to take more responsibility for this status quo — at which point they become co-teachers and co-learners.

Ask them what they appreciate, what their concerns are and what ideas they have for making improvements. Together, come to agreement about changes to try. Suddenly, students have a vested interest in making the class succeed. Through follow-up questions and ongoing interactions, you can enhance students' motivation, success, and learning.

There is no trick to establishing dialogue between students and instructors. Something as simple as a physical reorganization of the room can often be enough to get a better dynamic going in class. James Treat (American Studies) prefers that desks are arranged in a circle rather than rows so that everyone can see each other and have an equal voice in the discussion. Students know that when they arrive in his class, they are to rearrange the desks. This example may illustrate a minor point, but the principle is nonetheless important: here, students are not only treated as equals during class, they are physically responsible for their equal status as well. Such a small step toward inclusiveness, when combined with other small steps, can carry you and your class a long way.

Sociologist Dane Archer augments a class discussion on the detail and variety of body gestures in other cultures through the use of a videotape, which features foreign students from a local English as a Second Language class. Indeed, you may have some first-hand experience with a gesture that means something innocuous in one culture but is quite suggestive or derogatory in another.

> Your skills, behavior, and attitude in and out of class are, of course, major elements in setting the tenor of the environment, and while there is no substitute for being yourself, you can accent your own personality and style with a few overt expressions of common courtesy. Gini Matute-Bianchi (Education) combines intellectual energy with a deep concern for her students. Although her course content is laced with topical issues and her own style conveys a sense of urgency, she always shows a personal interest in their well-being. Despite the often rigorous pace of her class, she nevertheless takes time to stop what she is doing and ask about a student who is absent, or to encourage students who are facing big exams. By seeing them first as individuals, with lives of their own, she gets her students to respond in kind, treating her and each other with respect and concern.

Special Needs, Diversity, Empowerment, and Success

A related issue deserves to be taken up here, namely how we are to deal most constructively with special-needs students and their particular difficulties in the university. As students with special needs enter the university in increasing numbers, instructors must constantly look for ways — old and new — to help support learning when students struggle.

In classes where student well-being and satisfaction are clearly of concern to the instructor, and where students find their teachers willing to listen and empathize with them, differences in student heritage, lifestyles, as well as learning style, can become instructional strengths, where previously they might have been impediments. An atmosphere of mutual respect for racial, cultural, socioeconomic, and religious differences is not only crucial to success, it can also be a powerful tool for engaging students and helping them work better with others in class.

Another benefit of a more inclusive style of teaching is that students (as well as teachers) begin to discover that their own impressions not only can have a place in class discussions, but that they are valuable and valid responses to the material. Students can discover a spectrum of meanings in the same readings; they learn that singular truths about these readings may be impossible to support. Perhaps most importantly, they begin to gain a confidence in their own abilities to think critically and creatively. Beginning with a sense of being able to trust and act upon their own thoughts, rather than waiting for an authority to come and tell them why these thoughts are considered right or wrong.

Gender-Sensitive Teaching

Along with concern for culture, ethnicity, and disability, there is a great need to recognize the significance of gender in the classroom. Like issues of race, gender issues are not simply topics of discussion in the classroom, but matters which can intrude upon the teaching and learning processes because they are endemic to the culture. Unfortunately, discrimination doesn't disappear when we enter the gates of higher education, although it may be harder to perceive and overcome when it takes place in such an "enlightened" atmosphere. For that reason, we must all consider these issues carefully, scrutinize our values, and devote time and energy to righting past wrongs.

Recent research describes a disturbing loss of resilience among girls and young women when they enter puberty and face a primarily patriarchal world. Gilligan and others (1991) have theorized that personal and cultural disassociation becomes the normative pattern for girls who, as young adults, see their roles largely prescribed for them by men. As a result of this alienation from themselves and their role in the culture, they become afraid to assert themselves in places where they have learned that their opinions are unwelcome.

This anxiety can be devastating to a woman's chances of thriving in the classroom. As she tries to maintain her interpersonal relationships with peers

In the current political climate, where the pressure of diversity and inclusiveness may vie for class time with content coverage — especially in the Humanities — you as a teacher may walk a treacherous tightrope. Margo Hendricks (English Literature) brings her concern and appreciation for intellectual diversity to the structure of her classes and the choice of readings. As debate and discussion about the literary canon swirl around campuses, professional conferences, and publications, Hendricks is accepting of the change, but at the same time resists adopting any single alternative canon in her own teaching, working instead toward an overt and directed investigation of diversity and uniformity. In an area that until fairly recently has been very European and very male, her act of turning the notions of "canon" and "discipline" into topics of discussion stimulates discussion about diversity and empowerment among both students and colleagues. This is not to say that you should squelch your convictions in the classroom: just remember that you are an educator, and any partisanship you exhibit should be toward encouraging students to critically examine the issues as well as their own beliefs and feelings.

For example, in Hendricks' class on Renaissance drama, students are quick to appreciate the range of readings she has adopted, but just as important is their acceptance of the diversity of opinion that she promotes in class. To manage this, she resists any pressure toward closure and reductive truth. As she consciously removes the robe of Expert Authority and joins with students in a guided and largely nonjudgmental exploration of possible interpretations, she invites them to experience a new relationship with her, the other students, and the material. In this way, she avoids being a propagandist for a particular group, and instead encourages the class to explore their own prejudices and presumptions.

Dr. Gini Matute-Bianchi (Education) underscores the need for an inclusive classroom where everyone feels that they are a welcome participant. She proposes the following questions for instructors to answer with respect to their classes:

Do all students — regardless of race — participate actively and frequently, or is one particular group conspicuously silent?

Do you feel somewhat uncomfortable talking about issues of race and ethnicity when certain students are present?

Do you treat all students alike?

Is your teaching style culturally neutral, or does it favor students from a particular cultural background?

Do all students come to you for extra help when they need it?

These questions come from a longer list that Matute-Bianchi uses to promote self-reflection and discussion. As the provost of a college at a research university, she oversees the design and delivery of a required course, Values and Change in a Diverse Society, where the diversity of the incoming students intersects with course content to form a dynamic mix of personal opinion and academic theory. However difficult the challenge, Matute-Bianchi remains convinced that learning to deal effectively with diversity is a wonderful opportunity to grow as an instructor.

and with the teacher, and at the same time fulfill her perceived role in the culture, she may be driven to avoid an honest response which may be in conflict with her prescribed role as passive non-participant. Consequently, "I don't know" becomes an all too frequent response to questions for female students who have been encouraged to be docile.

When you hear this habitual form of non-response, it is a sign that you need to do more work to make class more accommodating and less intimidating for female students. As Gilligan points out, this dis-association becomes more problematic as adulthood progresses, and as the contrast between inner world and the outer facade comes into deeper conflict. Making a special and conscious effort to create a safe and inclusive class can do much more than make your semester run more smoothly: it may help save some of your students from pain later in life.

Unlike women, however, males have been socialized into (rather than out of) a largely patriarchal world (the amount of reading material written by men in the typical college course attests to the importance of the male voice in the university). Expectations for men from parents, siblings, and friends may be quite different. For example, rarely have men been subjected to the same degree of sexual intimidation and harassment as women may have. Consequently, a different set of concerns arises for male students: men must frequently be introduced to these issues from the other direction, namely how to identify gender inequity and what could be done about it.

One way for dealing with such issues is quite simple: don't ignore them. Address issues of cultural, racial, and gender discrimination openly, and take steps to promote a sense of connectedness among students. Watch for problems, and intervene before they become serious. Remember especially that behavior which might strike you as calculatedly malicious might actually be simply the actions of an ignorant student, oblivious to the effects of his or her behavior. Sometimes, a private, gentle talk after class is enough to avert further trouble.

Bettina Aptheker (Women's Studies) points out that both men and women have an inner world, and that giving expression to it is a vital part of education, and an important part of mental health generally. Encouraging students to speak honestly about their feelings builds the confidence necessary to bridge these inner and outer worlds and promote more holistic responses on the part of the student.

Aptheker calls upon all instructors to rethink their approaches to teaching in view of the emerging evidence that female students can be particularly disadvantaged in the traditional classroom, but she is quick to point out that the problem doesn't end there. Males, too, need an environment of acceptance in order to thrive intellectually. Like their female peers, they need to feel safe in class, encouraged to freely express their feelings and opinions.

Aptheker pays careful attention to the interactions among students in her classes and sets ground rules for discussions so that students will know, for example, how to handle interruptions or how to respond to expressions they perceive to be racist or sexist in class. Frequently, when these problems are aired openly, you will find that your students themselves will be able to address them with a surprising degree of sensitivity and sophistication.

Assessing the Climate for Learning

As you consider the climate in your own classes, you can ask yourself the following sets of questions with respect to the program, the process, and various materials needed:

PROGRAM

- What are your expectations for individual performance?
- Do you encourage students to ask questions and/or to express their personal viewpoints in class?
- Is there flexibility in what is required of students?
- Do students have a voice in what happens in class?
- In what ways do you help students to develop problem-solving abilities?
- Are you open to exploring a variety of learning approaches?

- Is instructional and programmatic support available for students who seek it?

PROCESS

- Are you interested in your students as individuals?
- Have you determined classroom rules and procedures cooperatively?
- Do you consult with students to identify educational goals?
- By what means do you and your students identify and solve conflicts?
- Are effective communications evident?
- Is everyone who is affected involved in decision-making?
- Do students have a sense of autonomy as well as a willingness to accept the accountability that goes with it?
- Are effective teaching-learning strategies evident?
- Is there an ability to plan for the future?

MATERIAL

- Does everyone arrive on time and prepared for class?
- Have you thought about the physical appearance and the comfort level of your classroom?
- How would you describe the physical atmosphere in your classroom?
- Can you have materials produced for class in a timely and convenient manner?

For each of these questions to which you are able to give positive answers, congratulate yourself. However, be careful not to conclude that negative answers are signs of failure; rather, look at them as signposts which — if you read them carefully — will lead you to a more effective and more rewarding teaching experience as student morale and learning intersect and increase.

In my own classes, I always want students to feel welcomed and cared for as individuals. If they find my classes interesting, enjoyable, and rewarding, if they believe they are learning meaningful material, then I always feel that I can ask a lot of them. I can challenge them, to think deeply about complex issues, to consider new and more creative possibilities and not just what may be on the next exam.

Because I want my students to be successful, I never grade on a curve any more. Indeed, I often remind them of how much I want all of them to successfully meet the standards set for the course; eg., 90% correct on exams for an "A." Because university tradition has often meant pressure on teachers for a "normal" distribution of grades, I do feel an obligation to be prepared to defend the criteria I set. However, after twenty years of teaching in higher education, I have yet to be called on that feared carpet.

Consequently, I invest time in and out of class to learn my students' names. I also want them to learn each other's names. Indeed, one of my hopes for each class is that students will feel comfortable enough to reach out to each other for support and assistance, to study together and help each other with drafts for papers. To encourage this process, I will regularly mix in small group activities, as well.

If time in class is positive and valued, attendance should be higher. On a more fundamental level, I also believe that I am making a valuable contribution to the field beyond the required knowledge, understanding and skills when their associations are primarily positive. Those positive feelings should then help support their ideals and carry them through those typically difficult first few years of adjustment and growth on the job.

I also want teaching to be fun for me. There is a vitally important infectiousness here which students at all levels identify as enthusiasm. Student morale affects my morale and vice versa. My desire to be effective energizes my preparation before class and my concentration during class. I do believe that a positive climate is energizing for everyone.

Being attentive to climate also means that I regularly solicit feedback from students, both formally and informally. I'll try to go to class early, in part to check with students about their progress and concerns. Likewise, I'll hang around after class to chat. In most classes I will also take some time at different points during the semester to solicit feedback, orally or in writing, about student likes, concerns, and recommendations for improvement. When I have done this for other teachers, students are always appreciative of the opportunity to express their opinions before the course is over.

I often feel that attention to climate increases my self-awareness as I look for clues of student engagement: eyes, body language, smiles, and comments. When combined with the active solicitation of feedback, I have more confidence that I have my finger on the pulse of class.

Bill Timpson

CORE CONCEPTS

Classroom climate

Morale and productivity linked

Shared responsibility

Special needs and accommodations

Diversity

Gender sensitivity

CHAPTER TWO

Other Issues for Learning

The difference between a teacher and a student is that the teacher knows it all and the student doesn't, right?

Not quite.

While you may know a lot more than your students about many things, that is not enough — your fundamental goal has to be their learning. Who hasn't had the terrible feeling of knowing a key concept or idea backward and forward, and knowing as well how important it is for students to grasp — and yet watching as student after student drops off or gives up? At those times, we know that being the expert is not enough.

Traditionally, it has been the case that "good professors" were those who were undisputed masters of their fields, who could be counted on to have a good answer for any question put to them, and who poured a ton of information into their receptive students semester after semester. Now, while expertise is certainly essential to teaching, it is only part of the answer. Today teachers must deliver an evolving subject matter to a student body which is itself evolving. The changing shape of institutions of higher education adds even more complexity. Creativity becomes a vital element of academic success in this context. And while having answers will continue to be the hallmark of experts, the ability to shape student thinking will always be the hallmark of the best teachers.

Paulo Freire's classic work, *The Pedagogy of the Oppressed* (1968), sounds a clear call for instructors to move from a traditional emphasis on the transmission of information — what he calls a "banking theory" of education, where facts are poured into a student's head — toward a greater focus on both political and intellectual liberation through critical thinking. When

This is an instance of how a teacher can use pacing to jump-start the minds of students, and to promote real engagement with the material. Writing instructor Susan Kimoto mixes her encouragement and support for students with a form of shock treatment. In both upper-division and lower-division classes, she requires the completed draft of a forty-page paper by the second week of class. The initial response from her students was also fairly predictable: "Forty pages! Impossible! "

After two weeks, students make an important discovery: it is possible for them to produce a forty-page draft, however rough that draft might be. Then, students work with Kimoto for the remaining eight weeks to develop and refine their ideas. By the end of the term, they have produced their papers. In working for many weeks on a single long paper, students experience the process of writing as most writers do, in all its iterative and messy phases. Indeed, Kimoto points out, this is how most manuscripts are refined for publication.

Her students learn to reread their original drafts carefully, looking for valuable ideas that can lead to the formation of a research question. At the same time, they learn to recognize and discard material that is not useful (an excruciating lesson, as any writer knows).

This approach has two benefits. First, students distribute their efforts across the entire semester — on a project that is undeniably theirs — rather than cramming all their work into the final two or three weeks. Second, students are immediately engaged, thrown into this seemingly impossible assignment, quickly bond with each other, offering much support and assistance. Once the course and the assignments are completed, most of Kimoto's students report a new self-confidence which allows them to complete lesser assignments in later courses with fewer self-defeating beliefs and presumptions.

the sole goal of education is to reproduce course material, teachers neglect the vast intellectual and personal reserves which students embody. Enormous opportunities for learning may be lost in the rush to cover course material, if you don't pay attention to *how* this material is being received.

When educational goals and styles shift toward learning environments which affirm personal freedom and growth, and harness the creative energy of students, the classroom can become a place of exciting discovery for everyone, which stimulates a rich intellectual life. This chapter will discuss some practical strategies for doing just that, for making students more active participants in the learning process, and not just receptacles of information.

Pace

While everyone believes that students need to be challenged intellectually, it is surprising how often we teachers find ourselves faintly apologetic for an ambitious class plan. Haven't almost all of us, at one time or another, assured our students that the material "really isn't all that difficult"? This sort of reassurance, however, can be misguided, since the message given is mixed.

Basically, we may be telling students: "Don't worry, you won't have to work hard on this class!" A much better approach might be a direct statement, "This class will require a great deal of work on your part." Try making this announcement, then see how many will rise to the challenge, and perhaps exceed everyone's expectations. Rallied in this manner, many of your students will become more engaged in the work being done, and much more willing to be co-authors of the curriculum.

Planning and Spontaneity

At the heart of the best teaching in higher education is the tension between the instructor's goals and students' motivations, abilities, and needs. Inevitably, when we are successful at challenging our students, we are stretching them to think and learn, to reexamine old ideas and master new material. Through the course of their postsecondary experience, students are expected to progress from simplistic and dichotomous thinking, to develop greater abilities to grasp complexity and appreciate multiple perspectives (e.g., Perry 1981).

Accommodating this tension is one of the great challenges of teaching, and while it would be terrific if we could simply make a place for it in our class plans, learning (and life) are rarely that easy. Indeed, in the successful classroom — where students are engaged, actively participating and learning — a great deal of what happens may be ad-libbed by the teacher in response to the shifting tides of the moment. This in turn can produce a companion tension between your careful advance preparation for teaching and the improvisation which may be necessary once class begins.

If course organization is flexible and concerns can be addressed collectively and responsibly, students will feel an increased sense of ownership for their own learning. By taking time during the semester to solicit feedback from students, for example, you can demonstrate an openness to your students' needs, ideas, and experiences. These course assessments, formal or informal, give students a chance to state what they like best about a course

> Some teachers seem to energize their students through the sheer excitement of the speed at which material is covered. Physics professor Dave Dorfan, for instance, teaches difficult material at a very demanding pace. Because physics courses have the reputation of being tough, Dorfan creates an expectation that students can succeed if they are willing to work hard. While offering encouragement as they struggle with the material, Dorfan often repeats his observation that the material is indeed difficult, but that by working together students can be successful.

Peggy Delaney (Marine Sciences) shifts easily between plan and improvisation. She dislikes the traditional, information-driven strategy for teaching science that has discouraged many talented students. Instead, she attempts to blend a careful organization of content with an alert sensitivity to student needs for clarification, assistance, and involvement. Delaney comes to each class with specific goals, yet is open to student questions and comments.

When nominated for her university's Innovation in Teaching Award, Delaney described her desire to move away from the "firehose" approach to teaching, where students are blasted non-stop with information. She points out that it is crucial to organize a lesson so that students have the opportunity to think in class, to be active and creative. In this kind of format, planning must incorporate need for spontaneity, and permit ongoing reorganization of coverage.

Physicist Joel Primack insists that guiding students toward insights about their own limitations and misconceptions can be much more effective than attempting to correct errors directly. Indeed, says Premack, guiding students to discovering their own misconceptions may be the only way to undo faulty thinking. Of course, this can be time-consuming and unpredictable, but why should it be otherwise?

and where they have concerns and to make recommendations for change. After receiving this input, you will then have the opportunity to make some changes before the end of the term. Your students will be appreciative, and if they feel better about you and the course, then you can ask and expect more: a real win-win opportunity.

Nurturing Risk-Taking

Another challenge for every instructor is to create a classroom environment which provides a foundation for risk-taking. If the students expect to extend themselves in your class, and know that they won't be punished for doing so (either by you or their peers), they will be much more willing to engage with the material and contribute actively in class. Any number of simple ways to promote feelings of mutual respect and trust between you and your students can encourage more active classroom experimentation. For instance, have students take turns standing with their arms folded and their eyes closed in the middle of a tight circle of five to eight people. One at a time, they fall forward or backward into the others, who gently catch them and then pass them along to someone else. For those who feel up to it, have them fall backward off a table into the linked arms of classmates. Another example of this kind of community-building exercise is a "trust walk," in which students guide blindfolded classmates around a building or up and down stairs.

Activities like these — while they may be greeted at first with snickers and some resistance and take some time — accomplish two goals for you. First, they build a sense of camaraderie among the students, enhancing class morale and the climate for learning. Second, such activities serve to break down inhibitions — once students do stunts like these, they'll think nothing of contributing their own ideas in class, or doing anything else you suggest. What a license and opportunity!

This sort of activity does not ensure, of course, that increased student participation will always be an obvious plus: digression, distraction, and repeat questions will be frequent. Keeping a good pace in class must be constantly balanced against the need to maintain an emotionally safe climate and a high level of student participation. When discussions do wander, you will have to intervene and get back on track without stifling students. If you have done a good job in nurturing a positive climate in class, the best way to proceed may be to say "We're digressing, and although this is interesting, we'll have to take it up out of class." You might close off an interesting avenue, but your class plan has to take precedence. There are no simple formulas here, only a commitment to learning; ultimately, you must rely on your professional judgment and the feedback you get from your students.

However, sometimes your students come up with things that are simply wrong, and the more open your classroom format is, the more this will happen. Hunter (1982, 87) points out that instructors need to learn how to "dignify" the errors that students make, trying to understand the thought-processes that led to a wrong answer, and then directing this thought in the right direction. If you tell your students that you value their contribution, and point out what may be valid

> The value of first impressions in the classroom is difficult to overestimate: getting off on the right foot can be critical to your teaching, as well as to your state of mind as a teacher. For that reason, I try to choreograph the first meeting of a semester very carefully, mixing the serious business of beginning a class with the lighter work of getting to know one another. One ice-breaking exercise that works well at the end of a first class meeting (especially in an introductory or first-year class) begins with arranging students in a circle, and then going around the circle, with students introducing themselves. However, instead of giving some fact about their life (major, hometown, etc.), they tell the class what fruit or vegetable they would be if they had the choice, and why. The selections are often hilarious, and the reasons even more so.
>
> The benefits of this exercise are two-fold. One, the necessary informality of this type of conversation as well as the constant laughter begins the semester in a surprisingly comfortable fashion; this comfort invariably infects the rest of the course. Two, I write the selected fruits next to the student names in my gradebook: the entry *Dorothy Vidalia onion* has proven to be a sure-fire method of matching names to faces, and remembering a little about the student's personality as well.
>
> *Paul Bendel-Simso*

in their mistakes, you'll be better able to say "That's wrong" to a student without it sounding like "You're stupid." Spending a little extra time on establishing this atmosphere in the beginning of a course can save time in the long run, since unacknowledged difficulties and confusions will be diminished and the time remaining will be of a higher quality.

Finally, take the time occasionally to find out how deeply a student may understand the material — probe some. Don't be afraid to push your students, to find out how fundamental their comprehension is. This will help you identify inadequacies and inaccuracies in your own assessments, since what you take for granted — what you assume they know — might be precisely the piece of information or idea which they lack. Challenge their understanding, determine at what point their knowledge gives out and where their understanding collapses. Confront opinions that seem ambiguous, and you will often turn student confusion into deeper comprehension.

Literature teacher Mary Kay Gamel is keenly aware of the engagement that a well-organized theatrical performance can inspire in an audience. To enhance her teaching, she regularly borrows techniques, approaches, and ideas from the theater.

Gamel believes that all instructors can profit from picturing themselves in a variety of roles related to the theater. As directors, they plan and conduct a class; as set designers, they pay attention to lighting, sounds, props, seating arrangements, and displays; as actors, they convey ideas through words, movements, expressions, gestures, and costumes.

Gamel notes that instructors sometimes get sidetracked in class by details that they find intriguing but which may be confusing to students. To avoid this, Gamel emphasizes the importance of pointing out the large, organizing concepts for students, and then using concepts as the "plot." To prepare physically, intellectually, and emotionally for teaching, Gamel also recommends warming up.

Transmission and Performance

There is an element of artistry to orchestrating a class successfully, and more often than not the kind of art you're performing is a species of theater. Just as actors must know their characters to portray them convincingly, so must instructors know their goals and objectives in order to teach effectively. The emotional aspect of any class is also of concern for the "theatrical teacher," and relates closely to the question of climate.

Theater people often use the expression "raising the stakes," which points to a simple truth about the stage: Unless both actors and audience are committed to a show, it will flop. The same is true for teaching and learning; if students remain uninvolved in the proceedings, even the best prepared class plan may fail. Teachers can "raise the stakes" in any number of ways, but in every case the key factor is to make sure that students feel the material matters to them. Once their own passion and excitement have been aroused, as well as your own, teaching can be just as exhilarating and just as much fun as theater. Each performance requires careful preparation, concentration, and professionalism, but the payoff is well worth the effort.

Because of the close parallels between teaching and the theater, you can always find an abundance of ideas and recommendations in the literature on performance skills and training. For example, two books — *Teaching as Performing* by Timpson and Tobin (1982) and *Teaching and Performing: Ideas for Energizing Your Classes* by Timpson, Burgoyne, Jones, and Jones (1996) — contain discussions of the parallels between the stage and the classroom, and provide an abundance of ideas and exercises for teachers. The skills of a university instructor to deliver material effectively influence both student engagement and retention: from vocal projection to clear enunciation, from gestures to movements that do not distract, actors study how their delivery affects the audience. The teacher can also improve by attending to these same skills.

Technology in the Classroom

Among the strategies you may wish to explore as you focus on improving engagement and climate are a variety of instructional technologies. Media that allow students to see real-world images of concepts under study can make instruction more concrete, comprehensible, and meaningful. Images and sounds can broaden, deepen, and reinforce learning, and you can often find very useful material in very ordinary places.

Most importantly, technology can revolutionize the climate for learning by allowing students to become more active in constructing their own education. If you ask students to write their own software or produce their own videotapes, for instance, or if you teach the use of spread sheets to display and organize data, you provide opportunities for students to think for themselves. You then become a facilitator, using your expertise less for transmission of information and more for guidance in learning. A good climate for learning can encourage greater trust and involvement which, in turn, can lead students toward the development of new skills.

In many ways, classroom innovation is inextricably linked to technology: both the current and as-yet-untapped impact of technology on postsecondary teaching and learning seem infinite. Generally, many of us wait for affordable user-friendly software for the classroom, but for those of us with the know-how and the energy, software development provides an exciting frontier of largely uncharted possibilities for learning.

Education teacher Laurie Edwards studies applications of technology to learning. She speaks excitedly about the results of a controlled experiment by Idit Harel (1991). Harel had fourth-graders create software to teach fractions to third-graders. Results indicated that the fourth-graders who worked on the design project outperformed other fourth-graders in control groups in three areas: programming knowledge and skill, general mathematics achievement, and knowledge of fractions.

Edwards has decided to explore applications of this research in her own university classes. In one course, "Designing a Computer-Based Learning Environment," she guides her students in designing software for instructional purposes. By asking students to learn by designing software to teach others, she finds that she is turning teaching on its head. Edwards believes that putting material in computational terms enhances student understanding — designing a program with the goal of teaching others forces them to look more deeply at the material.

Her approach, a novel form of peer tutoring, has much support in the literature on cooperative learning; e.g., Johnson and Johnson 1975; Ehly and Larsen 1980. Because these students are working on a project of their own choosing, they tend to put in a great deal of effort, especially because it will be seen and used by others, including their friends and classmates. The power of this approach is the way it taps the skills, talents, creativity, and energy of students.

Concluding Thoughts

While some methods for ensuring a positive climate are easily incorporated into any classroom, others take a great deal of time and effort, and this consideration brings up a question: to what degree will you have to sacrifice content coverage for the sake of student morale, motivation, and the potential for higher quality instructional time? That's a tough one which only you can answer.

Our recommendation is as follows: whenever your goal is to facilitate student learning, then time spent on climate issues is generally worthwhile, since coverage alone cannot ensure learning. In his introduction to *The Art and Craft of Teaching*, Christensen (1982, xiv) paraphrases the American poet Amy Lowell in describing the complex interactive process of teaching and learning: "Teaching is like dropping ideas into the letter box of the human subconscious. You know when they are posted but you never know when they will be received or in what form." Attention to climate represents an attempt to enhance the receptive capacity of the student's letter box, and whatever it takes to get them to open their letter box is going to be worth the effort.

Like the others, I can attest first-hand to the benefits of technology for teaching and learning. While at Colorado State University, I spent over a decade developing and field-testing the use of edited videotapes for distance education. Faced with a need to deliver graduate coursework to sites some distance from campus, I worked with a television production team to produce a variety of programs which feature teachers at different levels demonstrating specific concepts and approaches.

These videotapes have been invaluable for bringing more of the real world into my own classes on campus. I could show experienced teachers at work in their own classrooms with their own students. By editing carefully, I could then select scenes from different levels and subject areas and focus precisely on particular concepts and strategies. These videotapes were then assembled into three different sets of fourteen 30-minute tapes and combined with a student handbook as three graduate-level telecourses. Collectively, these telecourses have been broadcast several times nationally through Mind Extension University and Jones Intercable in Englewood, Colorado.

This work gave me valuable new insights about instruction, findings that have been reported by other researchers in a variety of publications. I learned firsthand the benefits of capturing on videotape examples of classroom teaching which modeled the concepts and strategies I was describing in class. At the same time, I learned more about the limits of instruction that occurs only via the spoken or written word.

In addition, I received invaluable feedback through my own exposure in front of the television cameras. By watching myself work, I was able to analyze aspects of my teaching: my organization and pacing, for example, or the ways I fielded questions or facilitated discussions. I really got to see myself as my students saw me. Finally, my students on campus also benefited from the materials that I developed for off-campus use.

For this work I also received the award of a networked computer lab from IBM to augment these distance learning efforts. Although this work was just beginning when I began a four-year extended leave from Colorado State University, I could envision numerous possibilities with computer-based assignments and ongoing electronic interaction among students and instructors.

Bill Timpson

EXERCISES

1. Try to recall a class which had a distinctly positive climate. Now think of a class where the climate was negative, depressed, judgmental, sarcastic, or the like. What was different about the instructors? The assignments? The other students?

2. Consider the determinants listed in Chapter One — program, process, and material. What changes could you make in any of these areas that might enhance the climate of your own class?

CORE CONCEPTS

Pace

Challenge

Planning and spontaneity

Nurturing risk-taking

Transmission and performance

Technology and climate

CHAPTER THREE

Development and Conceptualization

Development as the aim of education would indeed transform both educational theory and educational practice.

Wolfgang Edelstein
Effective and Responsible Teaching

In moving away from the "banking theory" of education, we acknowledge that while the knowledge and skills which we teach are vital, there is another essential objective at stake: attention to the intellectual development of students. Both learning and development are crucial aspects of student success in the classroom. In this chapter, we will investigate the nature of intellectual development, and discuss some of the practical lessons that can be drawn from an awareness of the process of mental maturation, and we will do it, as the chapter title says, through a dual consideration of cognitive development and conceptual learning.

It is widely accepted that the nature of human learning changes as individuals progress from infancy to adulthood. Developmental psychology points to distinct stages through which an individual passes on the way to full intellectual maturity, and at each stage, this individual manifests qualitatively different abilities and understandings. Typically, your students know less than you. However, if we place our traditional age college students on a developmental continuum, we can see that they often also think in simpler ways, that they are frequently more egocentric, that they rely more on their senses for understanding and decision making, etc. Mature adults are better able to think in more complex and abstract ways: they demonstrate greater sensitivity to perspectives other than their own, and they can better use symbols and abstract thought to supplement and organize sensory data. The writings of Tharp and Gallimore (1988), Rogoff (1990), Piaget (1952), Bruner (1966), Kohlberg (1963), Gilligan (1982) and Perry (1981) recognize these changes and challenge educators to rethink their instructional practices.

As a teacher in higher education, you may deal with a number of students who have done a great deal of growing up, but are not yet finished (neither are you, by the way!), and this presents a particular problem. Between childhood and adulthood, human learning proceeds gradually in a fixed sequence, but at vastly different rates in different people. The ramifications for teaching and learning are obvious: in situations where students demonstrate enormous variability in their readiness for learning, as well as great disparity in how much they know, you can become aware of these stages and adopt more appropriate teaching strategies, or else run the risk of losing a certain percentage of your students every semester. An awareness of these changes and a sensitivity to the course of intellectual development can help make you a more understanding and, therefore, more effective teacher.

Physicist Burt Jones displays an intuitive grasp of the fundamentals of developmental psychology in his introductory course on astronomy for non-science majors. Throughout the course, he makes frequent use of demonstrations to illustrate abstract concepts through concrete phenomena in class. In addition, he uses a constant flow of overheads to display pictures, drawings, graphs, and data sets as well as questions, comments, and summaries. These activities, plus his openness to questions, provide multiple and varied reference points and help students grasp new concepts and sort through complex ideas. Peter Scott (Physics) makes a point of encouraging students to come up after class to try out for themselves the devices he uses to demonstrate particular problems or concepts, ensuring that students have the opportunity to grasp new concepts by actually grasping them.

Leading Developmentalist: An Overview

Much of Jean Piaget's research (e.g., *The Origins of Intelligence in Children*, 1952) focuses on changes from infancy through adolescence as thinking gradually becomes less egocentric. Almost everyone has some acquaintance with ideas about child development, where visual clues dominate — an object put out of sight is assumed to disappear (i.e., object permanence) or a pipe cleaner bent is presumed to be shorter (i.e., conservation of length). But the development of the human mind doesn't stop here. As the adolescent matures into an adult, the mind develops a greater ability to think abstractly, use sophisticated logic, and handle complexity.

For those of us who teach at the postsecondary level, Perry's (1981) work on cognitive development is particularly illuminating. According to Perry, younger students at this level have a tendency to think in dualistic terms, to look for answers which are either right or wrong. This tendency is then reinforced by instruction that focuses primarily upon what the teacher or the text considers to be correct, and then uses objective, fact-oriented evaluation as the sole means of assessing progress. Over time and with challenging instruction, however, Perry reports that students can move toward a greater acceptance of intellectual complexity and alternative viewpoints. Ultimately, students are able to affirm their own commitments while respecting and evaluating the values of others.

In *Women's Ways of Knowing*, Belenky et al. (1986) argue that the process of helping students to find their own voices encourages intellectual change and maturation. They point out the importance of accepting the opinions of students without harsh evaluation as a way to foster learning and development. Similarly, it is important for you to reveal your own struggles in making meaning out of complex material, to share your own fears and concerns, false starts and insights. Former university instructor bell hooks (1988) describes this kind of learning in *Talking*

Nancy Stoller (Community Studies) mixes role-playing with debate in one of her classes to expose students to a broader range of opinion and foster a deeper level of understanding. For example, she had her students role-play a variety of characters from a broad political spectrum in a reenactment of the memorable Senate confirmation hearings on Clarence Thomas's nomination to the Supreme Court, during which Anita Hill brought charges of sexual harassment. Stoller's students were able to represent various characters and introduce a range of political stances, and the resulting diversity seemed to help students overcome the pressures to conform their political opinions to some acceptable norm. This approach helped to highlight the complexity of the case, and helped these students develop more empathy and understanding for those who think differently than they do.

This mode of teaching can also challenge you to explore new ways of assessing student knowledge and capabilities. Instead of relying solely upon the results of paper and pencil testing, you can draw conclusions about learning based on your own observations and conversations with students. Group projects, for example, provide a context in which you can watch and interact with students as they confront problems and consider solutions. Based on what you hear and see, you can then adapt subsequent lessons to better meet student needs. Group projects also provide students an active social context for learning.

Back. She finds this encouragement of voice especially important for African Americans, who have long felt suppressed and alienated in the U.S.

The ideas which result from this investigation by Belenky and her colleagues have deep implications for higher education, where students are often in the process of learning to develop hypotheses, reflecting upon their own thinking, and exploring alternative points of view. Your role here is to create the kind of stimulating environment that engages students actively and challenges their thinking. With a better understanding of the processes of learning and cognitive development, you can target instruction at an appropriate level of complexity and abstraction, not so far above them that students become lost, nor so simple that they are bored.

Jerome Bruner (1966) is one of the pioneers in the study of thinking, the ways of knowing that begin with infant exploration through touch, sight, and sound, and eventually evolve into abstract, language-mediated understanding. Bruner specifies three modes of learning which characterize human development to differing degrees from infancy through adulthood: the *enactive*, via physical touch; the *iconic*, via sight; and the *symbolic*, via language. Each of these three modalities continues to operate throughout life, the difference coming in the relative use we make of each. All three modes of learning may be important, depending upon the medium used. "Multimodal" teaching can tap all three, accommodating any learner's differing strengths or preferences. You can enhance this understanding, for instance, by supplementing lecture presentations with periods of active discussion, relevant audio-visual materials, small group cooperative projects, and/or independent practice.

Moral Development

The ethical considerations of any field provide wonderful opportunities for challenging the ways in which students think. If you need material that can prompt debates, for example, look to the dilemmas faced by teachers and students over grades, cheating or plagiarism, or over relationships that become conflicted or intimate. Here, the work of developmentalists like Kohlberg and Gilligan provide guidelines for very engaging instruction.

Building off the pioneering work of Piaget, Kohlberg (1963) proposes a developmental hierarchy of moral thinking that offers teachers another way to challenge student thinking. As in Piaget's model, we find a shift from the egocentric and toward the logical. Kohlberg's three stages and six levels of moral thinking have applicability for a wide variety of issues, including concerns about public policy, ethics, or even classroom dynamics.

Kohlberg's Stage Theory of Moral Reasoning

Preconventional Stage	
Stage 1	Thinking is shaped by a desire to obey or to avoid punishment. Students follow your directions without question; many may do so to avoid a poor grade.
Stage 2	Reciprocity is the key here. Motivation is sparked by what is expected in return. Students help each other with the expectation that they themselves will get help later.
Conventional Stage	
Stage 3	Being seen as good or nice; getting the approval of others. "Good" students are attentive, motivated, and courteous and hope thereby, to win the favor of their teachers.
Stage 4	Desire to maintain law and order. Students accept the need for rules.
Postconventional Stage	
Stage 5	Living with a social contract, preserving individual rights as codified in the U.S. Constitution.
Stage 6	Living by universal ethical principles and individual conscience. Christ, Gandhi, Martin Luther King, Jr.

Preconventional Stage

At level one, individuals respond out of a fear of punishment or a commitment to obedience. For example, what stops more students from cheating? Is it fear of getting caught or a principle about honesty? At level two, individuals manifest an instrumental relativist orientation; that is, they are concerned about reciprocity or what is self-serving. One student will help another in hopes of getting something in return.

Conventional Stage

At level three, individuals reason in terms of interpersonal concordance, or what pleases others. As a teacher, your approval may be very important to some students. At level four, individuals are concerned with the maintenance of law and social order. For instance, demonstrators on campus are expected to abide by certain rules and regulations.

Postconventional Stage

At level five, individuals respond according to a concern for a social or legalistic contract; they recognize that rules and laws serve social functions and can be altered. During the 1960s many college students joined in protesting those laws which upheld segregation. At level six, individuals live, act, and think according to self-chosen universal ethical principles. Some idealistic students fully accepted the nonviolent tenets of Ghandi, for example, and were willing to risk jail when protesting the war in Vietnam.

It is important to note that Kohlberg's model is controversial. The focus on values, the nature of the stages themselves, and their relationships to each other have all been challenged. The theory can nonetheless be helpful as a vehicle for assessing and challenging student thinking. When discussing the issue of political correctness, for example, less mature students may respond in terms of perceived effects: the consequences of being punished by a teacher for unpopular views (stage 1) or the benefits of popularity with peers (stage 3). Instructors, in turn, may err by missing these dynamics and assume that the class is following a free and more principled inquiry (stage 6). Knowing about Kohlberg's hierarchy can help you frame questions and guide discussions which reveal underlying beliefs and promote thoughtful self-analysis and reevaluation.

However, there is more here. Having defined the levels of moral development, Kohlberg then goes one step further and posits that students may not be able to understand reasoning more than one level above their own. If he is right about this, traditional instruction may indeed miss the mark at times. A more effective approach would be to pose open-ended questions, to listen carefully in an effort to assess the levels of students' responses, and then pitch your questions and prompts there or one level above. Highly principled comments may, unfortunately, fall on deaf (cognitively blocked) ears.

Consider, for example, the case of a student you suspect of cheating on an exam. Sensing the developmental stage of the student, you could vary your opening comments accordingly. For a student at stage one, you might say, "You realize there are consequences?"; at stage two, "How will this look on your permanent record?"; at stage three, "What do you think your friends will say if this gets out?"; at stage four, "There are good reasons for rules about cheating"; at stage five, "Do you value honesty?"; at stage six, "What principles do you live by?"

The Kohlberg model may be helpful for new staff taking a look at their own approaches to instruction. Their eagerness to be liked by their students (stage 3), for example, may cause them to lose sight of the importance of maintaining high expectations. Inexperienced teachers may also lack perspective on the rights (stage 5) that individual students have to a safe, orderly, respectful, and challenging classroom environment (stage 4) or the principles (stage 6) upon which they choose to run their classes.

To stimulate moral development, Kohlberg advocates discussion of dilemmas to force students to take positions and defend them. The classic dilemma concerns Heinz, whose wife is dying. A local druggist has developed a remedy, but he is demanding a high price. Heinz can only raise half the money required. The druggist will not lower his price. Should Heinz steal the drug? Why or why not? Once the dilemma is presented, students can be asked to write down their responses to the questions and small groups with similar views can be formed. Within each group, students can then share their responses and try to reach consensus about the most important reason, the next most important, and so on.

According to Kohlberg, this activity alone can stimulate rethinking and moral growth as students wrestle with arguments at different levels. Later the larger group can reassemble and join in a structured debate. The teacher plays a critical role here in maintaining the focus on one line of argument at a time, in guiding the discussion back and forth between opposing sides for statements, clarifications, and rebuttals. Where and why student opinion differs gradually becomes apparent to all. The dissonance that is created as individuals are exposed to arguments at higher levels can be a catalyst for developmental growth.

In her provocative book, *In a Different Voice*, Carol Gilligan (1982), a former member of the Kohlberg research effort, raises some fundamental questions about the universality of these developmental models, arguing that the works of Piaget, Kohlberg, and others may, in fact, have predictive value primarily for white males living in Western societies. While analyzing research protocols, Gilligan ran into difficulty as she attempted to categorize female responses within Kohlberg's hierarchy.

According to Gilligan, women consistently used reasoning that did not clearly fit anywhere within Kohlberg's model. Many of her female subjects wanted to talk about primary relationships and how these would be affected by particular decisions. In the case of Heinz's dilemma, for instance, what would happen to his wife if he should steal the drug, be caught, and punished? Could they afford the risk of extended separation, especially while his wife was in pain and needed him for support and comfort? Whereas males tended to argue about legalistic and ethical considerations, females often thought more about relationships and the effect on others. Gilligan has raised similar concerns about the universality of Piaget's system, which describes an increasingly logical orientation to thinking and ignores other ways of knowing and deciding.

Applying a Developmentalist Perspective

As you can see, a developmentalist focus on your teaching can increase your chances of reaching more students. All students can be challenged to think critically, to integrate new material efficiently into what they already know (assimilation) or alter those ideas which are no longer valid or useful (accommodation), to utilize increasingly sophisticated logic and abstractions to handle complexity and ambiguity. At the same time, teachers can do more to design stimulating environments and facilitate active learning.

Awareness of these developmental changes and issues can help you "lure" students into deeper learning and critical thinking with lessons that promote hands-on, active, and experiential learning. In this way you can "teach" less and observe more, watching for useful indicators of capability and progress. By probing student thinking, especially their errors, you can find fresh insights into the underlying processes of learning, and thereby refine your teaching strategies.

While the idea of individualizing instruction might seem overwhelming, an appreciation for developmental stages may help you adapt more of your curricula and teaching strategies to meet individual student needs. In any situation, providing the opportunity for many different kinds of learning can help you accommodate various developmental stages and learning styles — the individualization of instruction will be done by the students themselves: for one student, the hands-on approach may be the best way to learn, while the next student learns best by carefully working things out mentally, without ever picking up an instrument. By watching carefully, you can find which methods work for which students; your task is to make sure that what you're offering is what they can use.

A successful use of a developmental orientation in teaching requires you to place greater emphasis on student interaction and responsibility to think and learn; this means that classroom climate and open communications are crucial. Once you manage to encourage more student-centered and student-driven forms of learning, both you and your students will begin to see some of the restrictions and limitations of the traditional instructor-dominated approach.

Readiness

Can this development be accelerated or must a teacher wait patiently for a student to be ready? The answer from the developmentalists is ambiguous. Whereas they regularly advocate the creation of stimulating environments and challenging assignments which engage students actively, they also acknowledge that the degree and pace of learning will typically vary from one person to another. Some students demonstrate quick mastery. Others require second and third explanations before finally understanding. Some may need alternative teaching approaches. Most students benefit from practice and periodic review. Despite everything, a few may continue to struggle.

The one recommendation we have for you is to stay open to the variety of paths different students may need to maximize their own learning. "Staying open" may sound a bit fuzzy but two intriguing books about physics help to illustrate this more intuitive approach to discovery. In Zukav's *The Dancing Wu Li Masters* (1979) and Capra's *The Tao of Physics* (1991), you can find compelling arguments for a less prescriptive approach to research (and, we would argue, teaching) where insights occur when explorations flow (i.e., non goal-oriented) and researchers stay open to new possibilities. At core, physicists must face up to the humbling task of challenging what they don't know and deciding how to best teach what they know they don't know. While confusing at best, one way forward is to expect less from purely rational analyses and more from nonrational or intuitive insights. Think about it; or better yet, check in with your own intuition.

Even if one could assume equal ability among all students, developmental readiness and rate of learning will vary among individuals. In the case of students who are simply not quite ready, you may need to temper your impatience, keeping in mind that some of this process is simply out of your control. Some students may catch on during the semester. Some may not, no matter what you do. For practical purposes, however, one thing remains certain: by paying attention to student development, you will undoubtedly help many succeed who would have otherwise failed. Education and learning must be a responsibility which you share with your students.

Teachers and Their Development

Just as important in a discussion of student development are the changes that faculty members undergo across their professional careers, changes which inevitably affect their relationships with students, what they know about their discipline and what they bring to their teaching. We find the writings of Erikson (1974) and Levinson (1978), in particular, compelling in their descriptions of adult development. For example, several questions come immediately to mind: How does the career focus of young faculty members, especially at research universities, affect the energy and creativity they can bring to teaching? When teachers evolve through their own inevitable life transitions, what will change about their teaching, their relationships with students? Can senior faculty be used better to fulfill their "natural" inclination to mentor younger teachers? In our historic press to transmit knowledge and cover content, do we overlook the influence of development for both students and ourselves? We think so.

Conceptual Learning

What can be more fundamental to higher education than helping students think clearly about complex systems and issues? Here is where the second part of the title to this chapter comes in. "Conceptual learning" is what we use to describe the processes by which students learn how to better organize information in logical mental structures, how to challenge ideas in light of new data, how to reorganize information and hypothesize new explanations, how to make sense of the swirl of news on this fast-shrinking planet, how to separate opinion from fact. It is the process by which human beings learn how to best understand the world around them. The challenge for teachers is to guide this development in such a way that students become increasingly skilled at thinking about their own thinking.

When we discuss *concepts*, we are talking about the organizing principles for critical thinking — the cubby holes in which the mind organizes facts into ideas. Simply put, conceptual learning is the ability to build these cubby holes; it's a skill that human beings can develop and refine throughout their lives. In their classic work, *A Study of Thinking* (1967), Bruner, Goodnow, and Austin define *concepts* as categories capable of including an unlimited number of instances with certain common characteristics, and they describe *concept attainment* as the process of identifying attributes that distinguish instances from non-instances in any particular case.

In both Piaget's and Bruner's models, group discussions and multiple viewpoints are important catalysts to move students beyond egocentric, physicalized orientations and to develop more abstract reasoning capabilities. Translated into the classroom, this means that intellectual diversity within any class or group — which some teachers see as a burden — can be reframed as a valuable resource, a catalyst for challenging students to think at more advanced levels.

When this happens, two fundamental processes occur. First, students attempt to *assimilate* new information into their existing mental schemata; i.e., they place new facts into their current world-view. Second, they attempt to change these schemata to *accommodate* information or ideas which do

I recently had first-hand experience with this kind of evolving understanding when I took a calculus course in an effort to fill one of the gaps of my undergraduate education. Throughout the semester, I was frequently surprised to see how clearly one could tell the differences between an effective and useful lesson plan, one that wasn't going quite as well, and those that were frank catastrophes. Almost without exception, the good class periods began with a clear articulation of goals for the hour, an explanation of the value of mastering this goal, and a well-paced derivation of the new knowledge from prior lessons. If any of these elements were missing, or if the instructor failed to notice when his work at the chalkboard was bewildering to his students, the class promptly fell apart.

When I felt it would be courteous and useful to do so, I took advantage of my dual status as peer and student to talk with the instructor about some of his unconscious habits as a teacher. It turns out that his "math brain" (unlike mine) had trouble understanding the difficulty most students have with the concepts of the derivative and the integral. Both his natural intelligence and long experience made calculus appear so intuitive and natural to him that he had trouble suppressing his impatience with the often slow progress of the students. As a consequence, he often felt that he had to speed up the class in order to compensate for the students' slowness — this solution was understandably problematic! In addition, he was fascinated by the intricacies of mathematics, and brought his love for the subject into the class in the form of frequent digressions. He felt justified by the beauty of the mathematics involved, but didn't realize that the students were generally panicked by the flurry of numbers and symbols that he presented to them; to compound the problem, this digressive information often involved higher-level mathematics than we were learning at the time.

For this particular class, the answer to everyone's problems was fairly straightforward: the teacher needed to pay close attention to the pace of instruction, keep digressions to a minimum (while announcing them as such when they did arise), and keep open the lines of communication between students and teacher. Once the class felt comfortable saying "Stop! You're not making sense!" in the middle of a class period, teacher and class were much more able to work together toward common ends — tearing through the course curriculum during class, instead of tearing out our hair afterward.

Paul Bendel-Simso

not fit. Here they are motivated by a desire to maintain mental *equilibrium;* i.e., they develop new concepts to accommodate irrefutable data. Any time your students are learning something, one of these processes is going on, or possibly both. As education and learning evolve, as language and logic develop, these schemata should be able to accommodate increasingly complex and abstract concepts.

Cognitive development and conceptual development are distinct entities, but they are intimately linked: they stand as two components of a learning process that begins at infancy, and continues on throughout life. Their interaction is dynamic and evolving, with the developing mind accommodating more that is cognitively abstract and complex, which in turn allows more information to be processed into concepts, which then promotes a greater cognitive capacity to accommodate complexity, and so on. In short, the mind will develop best when challenged and guided toward creating and constructing that which is most meaningful.

Asking students to make sense of the world, to learn how to organize raw data as well as rethink existing paradigms (concepts, explanations, hypotheses), is central to good teaching, and especially important in higher education. As McKeachie (1990, 233) points out, "Much higher education involves developing a more specialized form of a structure than most students already have. Often teachers fail to help students see the link to the general schema they already know."

Teaching Concepts

In a discussion of intended learning outcomes for college students, Menges (1981, 559) lists conditions for complex cognition, including objectives which you may find useful as you think about the challenge of teaching concepts:

- The learner *demonstrates prerequisite knowledge* (memory).
- The learner *discriminates correct and incorrect examples* of concepts or concept chains. Problems should include correct and incorrect examples of increasing subtlety and variety.
- The learner *applies principles to new problems*. These problems should require students to modify previously used principles — dealing both with subject matter content and the process of learning — or generate new ones.
- The learner *practices problems* which can generate cognitive strategies and *receives relevant feedback*.

A good example of this schema is the way that calculus is often taught. By working on a series of examples, students eventually arrive at a certain conceptual understanding: they learn to recognize common themes which run through the different examples. In time, they learn how to apply these concepts more broadly without having to derive them anew each time. This kind of conceptual learning calls for students to respond to new situations by classifying, analyzing, synthesizing, and then applying ideas and information. As the teacher, your job is to arrange the class in such a manner that your students have enough raw examples to work on, but be sure that you do not introduce dissonant material or "exceptions" before your students have gained an understanding of the rule itself.

Higher-Order Rules

Gagné (1985) offers another description of skills for you to consider as goals and markers in the development of thinking. Discrimination, the ability to distinguish the identifying characteristics of an object, is a prerequisite for concept formation. Concepts, in turn, can be interrelated through rules, and rules can be combined into more complex higher-order rules. When students become familiar with this hierarchical way of organizing concepts, they can develop an intellectual sophistication and flexibility that is relatively permanent and that can be applied across disciplines.

In counseling psychology, for example, we could imagine using Gagné's hierarchy to conceptualize client-centered therapy where students are initially asked to distinguish among those responses which could encourage people to reflect inwardly. Various rules — use of reflective responses, attending behaviors, continuing responses, empathy — can be combined to create the desired therapeutic climate of acceptance, support, and hope (higher-order rule).

In physics, for example, one higher-order rule describes the effect of a force in producing an equal and opposite reaction. To really understand what these terms mean to a physicist, students typically start by learning first how to distinguish between acceleration and speed or velocity, and then how to combine this understanding with rules about mass to formulate higher order rules; e.g., force is equal to mass times acceleration (F=ma). Yet, cautions physicist Sandy Kern, his best teaching rarely proceeds in a linear, sequential manner beginning with what seems to be the most logical first step. Most often, his best first step means beginning with whatever understanding (flawed as it might be) students bring to class and then moving up and down the Gagné (1985) hierarchy as needed, dismantling misconceptions and then reconstructing the students' knowledge base according to the desired higher-order rules.

In my classes, I often ask students to describe the best examples of teaching from their own experiences. This activity challenges them to reflect and evaluate, to begin thinking about what has worked for them and why. It challenges me to facilitate a process where students are active and engaged, where everyone can participate and discover the extent of their agreement with others. At the beginning, I have students tell their individual stories while I list the most essential factors on the board. By grouping similar responses and adding labels, we then begin to hypothesize more generally about the most important characteristics of good instruction as derived from the collective experiences of those participating.

After we complete this process, I often display an overhead summarizing some of the academic research on effective teaching and compare its conclusions with the ones generated by the class. Through this kind of process, students address the issue of effective teaching in a manner which makes the concepts under review so much more memorable because of the grounding in their own experiences. It's great fun for me, too — lively, unpredictable, dynamic. Yes, I have to start the process and provide the initial rationale (fuel), but the way students get hooked into the discussion is also energizing for me.

When all the comparisons are finished, I also like to take a step back and briefly discuss the process with students; ie., what worked well, what didn't and why. This kind of debriefing process can strengthen the learnings and help cultivate more self-awareness about the thinking process — what psychologists will term metacognition or thinking about thinking. Hopefully, my students will learn something about effective group processing and various cooperative activities over the course of the semester.

Bill Timpson

In history education, there are similar hierarchies where higher-order rules can be used to explain particular events. Yet how would you resolve the following: while warfare has long consumed historians of every culture, the study of peace has always been problematic. Just how does one study the absence of war and conflict? Indeed, very little seems known about those forces which promote peace. What could students be asked to distinguish? What are the economic forces at play (rules)? The demographic or geographic rules? How do these interrelate in higher-order rules?

Rule-Example Rule

For his part, Slavin (1991) describes two different approaches to gaining an understanding of concepts: definition and observation. When learning by definition, students act as passive receptors of new knowledge while their instructor defines the concept for them, provides instances and noninstances, and then restates the definition. This pattern has come to be known as *rule-example-rule*, and it is the way that concepts are usually taught. By choosing examples of a concept carefully and presenting them sequentially, teachers can orchestrate a lesson to focus student attention on significant factors. Because the instructor provides all the information for students to absorb during such a presentation, it is termed a *declarative* teaching strategy.

Inductive Thinking

In contrast to the declarative approach is learning by *observation*, where students infer the definition of a concept from examples and nonexamples provided by the instructor. This method of conceptual learning requires students to think inductively, to formulate ideas from examples and to construct defensible explanations. Also known as a data-driven or bottom-up approach, it requires active student learning. Because many who teach at the university are familiar with an inductive approach through their own research endeavors, learning to teach concepts this way can feel quite natural.

In contrast to the deductive approach, which begins with a single concept or principle and moves toward relevant specifics, you can start an inductive approach with unorganized data and move toward a meaningful conceptual framework that connects the data and explains how they fit together. This process of concept formation helps students understand how information can be categorized, labeled, recategorized, and interrelated. Indeed, the inductive approach can demonstrate for students how conclusions will vary with the kinds of categories and labels that are established and how a conclusion — and all knowledge, for that matter — is fundamentally tentative.

Students begin the inductive process with raw data or disorganized information which their teacher has provided or that they themselves have generated from their own research on or knowledge of a particular topic. As the teacher, your role in inductive concept formation is to guide students as they attempt to group similar items together. Conclusions may vary as a consequence of how information is organized at this initial stage. Once grouping has occurred, you then assist students in finding appropriate labels for each category. Next, you can ask students to discuss the relationships among the various groups, and focus on how they interact and affect each other. Finally, you can help students venture predictions and design experiments to test their hypotheses.

Instructional technology can also play an important part in the development of an ability to conceptualize. When students use spread sheets to enter and organize raw data, for example, they have at their disposal tremendous power and an opportunity to make real sense of the world. They can learn to analyze the information available to them, draw conclusions based on the data, and put their own spin on the results.

Organized this way, the concept-formation process will inevitably be divergent, proceeding in any number of directions from the same data base, generating different conclusions that reflect the ways that different students organize and interpret information. Here is a summary of steps you can use to guide students in the process of concept formation (inductive thinking):

1. Provide or generate data
2. Separate data into categories and label
3. Analyze interrelationships among categories
4. Develop hypotheses that explain relationships
5. Test hypotheses

The inductive approach to concept formation really does challenge students to participate actively in the development of understanding. It invites them to think critically as they process unorganized information, to look for structure, and to consider various conclusions. Because there are often many ways to interpret any specific set of data, students benefit from hearing what others are thinking. Suddenly knowledge is demystified. Conclusions become more of a reflection of the way in which the data is organized and labeled, and less some ordained bit of truth.

The interactive, social nature of the process also makes it possible to accommodate and challenge students who are at differing levels of ability or who prefer different approaches. The early stages — grouping and labeling — work especially well with concrete learners, while the later stages — identifying interrelationships and creating explanatory hypotheses — are engaging for abstract thinkers. For visual learners, you could create an informational grid with descriptions arrayed on one side (e.g., the best teachers) and the derived categories listed across the top (e.g., knowledge, personality, climate, group skills).

Whenever you use the inductive approach, you will play a very active role as you lead students from the concrete toward the abstract, from active manipulation to reflection. In this way, you challenge students to think through complex issues and develop their own hypotheses. You serve as a conceptual guide and process facilitator as learning evolves. Whatever the topic, unexpected ideas will emerge for the discussions, challenging you and your students, and sending you in intriguing new directions. As students grapple with the process, you may wish to take advantage of the opportunity to step back and watch it unfold. Because this approach calls upon students to verbally organize and express their thoughts, you can assess understanding along the way, providing feedback or modeling the kinds of thinking you want to see on exams, for example.

A sociologist might give students an assignment to analyze raw, unorganized census data. Proceeding inductively, students first discriminate among various features of the data in order to establish groupings and then label these as categories, such as age, geography, income, and ethnicity. Then they move on to interrogate the hypothetical interrelationships between and among these categories. What, for example, is the relationship between age and place of residency in a particular community? Do senior citizens tend to live in certain areas? Students can suggest public policy recommendations based on their hypotheses. They may suggest, for instance, that housing for seniors be dispersed throughout the community rather than concentrated in one area. As the teacher, you can also point out how interpretation of any data set will inevitably reflect its initial grouping.

Inductive lessons also reveal that *thinking* as an activity is just as subject to personal habit and style as a person's gait or manner of speech: as with anything else, there are individual approaches to thinking. Bruner, Goodnow, and Austin (1967) propose a thinking-style continuum stretching from *impulsive* learners on one end to *systematic* learners on the other. The former tend to be more intellectually aggressive, often relying upon guessing as their dominant strategy. Such people might improve their chances for success by learning to make educated guesses. Systematic learners are more deliberate and more reflective. They typically approach conceptual learning carefully, trying to determine how various examples are similar and then identifying their critical attributes. These individuals progress in their learning by taking calculated risks.

As mediator, you must become aware of these different thinking styles. Because students also benefit from a broader and deeper understanding of their own thinking, it is worthwhile to take a few moments after any activity that involves conceptual learning to focus on the process, helping students understand their own tendencies as well as ways to consider alternatives. This part of the lesson is known as debriefing: here you can offer yourself as a model for students, sharing your own thinking as well as describing false starts and frustrations, insights and successes.

Like other active learning strategies, the inductive approach to conceptual learning requires more class time than the traditional declarative approach. On the positive side, it offers variety, an alternative to the routine of lecture, and increases the chances of engaging more students. You get to address critical and creative thinking, promoting metacognitive self-awareness (i.e., learning more about how to learn). As students engage actively in the acquisition of knowledge, they discover new ways of thinking about thinking, an awareness which will serve them well throughout their lives. That your students share responsibility for learning may be entirely new to them. An inductive approach can bolster students' preparation for class by challenging them to play a more active role during class and demonstrate the kinds of thinking you want to see on essay exams, for example.

Systematic attention to how students think about concepts can also elevate the quality of your instruction, sharpening your own thinking and questioning skills. At first you might concentrate on helping students to distinguish relevant from irrelevant attributes, but then move toward helping them discern the connections among concepts which produce general principles. Facilitating all this will keep you on your toes. Through the debriefing process you also get to hear what was especially valuable for students, what didn't go over so well, and get some hints for direction for future classes.

There is a pointed example of how effective an inductive approach to conceptual learning can be. A junior high math teacher served in a role that was termed the *naive expert* (Timpson and Jones 1989) because she had a firm grasp of the conceptual nature of mathematics, yet was naive about the capabilities of primary-aged students. Using an inductive lesson as a hierarchy (i.e., labeling, seeing interrelationships, and drawing inferences), the naive expert took first and second graders as far and as fast as she could in the time she had available. The regular classroom teachers, observing the process, noted which students thrived and which were frustrated. They also got to see which students appeared to be at higher cognitive levels of thinking. The teachers were generally amazed at what their children were able to do and how far they could go with an inductive approach. They had to rethink what "intelligence" really meant to them: some of their "best" students really struggled when given little guidance on new problems, while other, less disciplined students seemed to rise to the challenge. At the postsecondary level, the inductive model offers a wide range of "experts" as resources for the creation of challenging assignments: the entire faculty, other staff, and community resources can be your allies.

As a footnote to this section, we want to point out that the best tools for the development of the mind are often right at hand, and in the case of writing as a thinking exercise, this is quite literally true. Writing can be a powerful tool for developing critical thinking abilities, and certainly one of the cheapest and most effective technologies at our disposal as teachers. As the coordinator for a University's Writing Across the Curriculum Program, Ginny Draper works with faculty in various disciplines, calling upon them to recognize the essential role of practice in writing if students are to learn how to think. Thinking is required for students to become thinkers, she insists, and writing is a tangible method of formalizing the thinking process. If they only receive information passively, students will not learn to think critically or creatively. Draper calls upon teachers to sponsor, encourage, and help students refine thinking from the very first day of class, particularly through writing assignments.

Draper goes on to make a distinction between formative writing, which involves thinking and understanding on the part of the writer, and formal writing, which attempts to communicate with others. The type of writing assignment undertaken by students should reflect the specific objectives you have as a teacher. As you search for writing assignments, Draper encourages you to consider the kinds of writing you do in your own fields.

In addition, Draper is a great advocate of writing groups. Correcting written assignments can be both labor- and time-intensive for you. Many teachers will also complain about the difficulty of trying to comment on the content in a paper when writing skills are poor. Writing groups allow students to come together to talk about their writing and to give each other feedback during the process of writing so that their final draft is that much more refined.

Charles Atkinson of the Writing Program at the University of California-Santa Cruz has pioneered a peer writing program that trains students to help others in classes where assistance is needed. Student writing assistants in a seminar with Atkinson spend an entire quarter together studying the elements of writing improvement. They consider everything from organization to substance to style, from the needs of students new to the university to those in upper divisions, from the requirements of different disciplines to the concerns of the faculty. With the support of an instructional improvement grant, Atkinson guided a small group of writing tutors in the development of a manuscript for student writing assistants entitled *Walk a Fine Line* (1992).

EXERCISES

1. Teach a lesson based on Heinz's dilemma. Or create your own dilemma, and then focus on the ensuing discussion among students, noting which stages (Kohlberg) and concerns (Gilligan) you are able to identify.

2. Consider your own learning strengths, styles, or preferences. What is the best mixture of visual, auditory, and kinesthetic for you? What is the best mix of concrete and abstract? Has it always been this way? Are you aware of the preferences of your students? Are they much different? What does this mean for your teaching?

3. Look through Dan Levinson's *Seasons of a Man's Life* or Gail Sheehy's *Passages* for markers of adult development. These would be analogous to development in the cognitive and moral thinking domains as outlined in this chapter. Do any of these stages have applications in your teaching?

4. Consider a body of information in your own discipline. How did scholars first approach this information? What other interpretations are possible? Develop a lesson based on new information that needs organization.

5. Pair up with another instructor and observe each other as you both try out the inductive approach to conceptual learning. During the debriefing session with students, invite the observer to participate.

CORE CONCEPTS

Intellectual development

Rate of maturation

Learning styles or preferences

Active learning

Social context
- assimilation
- accommodation
- equilibrium

Moral development

Assessment and appropriate instruction

Complex cognition

Learning by definition and observation

Concept formation (inductive) or attainment (deductive)

Concept analysis or attainment

Debriefing

PART II

Teaching Strategies

CHAPTER FOUR

Preparing to Teach

Teaching does make a difference. It induces students to demand more of themselves, leads them to new ways of solving problems, and awakens unsuspected talents. It can inspire them to become more caring, creative, and thoughtful. But it can only do all this if done well.

James Wilkinson
Varieties of Teaching

If you are a teacher, and if you're reading this book right now, you are probably of the opinion that your teaching makes a difference: this fundamental belief in the value of what Wilkinson calls the structured dialogue between instructor and student may be one of the greatest assets you have. In the opening chapter of *The Art and Craft of Teaching* (1982), Wilkinson describes teachers as the intermediaries between students and a body of knowledge. By providing a structure within which learning can flourish, by giving feedback and support to students, you become a catalyst for growth and development, helping students stretch beyond their own self-imposed limits toward deeper understanding and more creative expression. Part II of this book provides a practical overview of various teaching strategies which can help you do this.

Every university teacher knows that no two classes are ever exactly the same. As the intellectual and emotional requirements for teaching and learning interact to produce a constantly changing set of circumstances, you make countless conscious and unconscious decisions in the course of every class. Some of these decisions relate to the material being presented:

- What major points will I make today?
- How do these relate to the material that has gone before?
- In view of the time spent answering questions, can I afford to treat the next topic in the time that remains?

Other decisions pertain to the teaching/learning process:

- How can I introduce this topic most effectively?
- What can students add?
- What means can I use to engage them in thinking about it?
- How can I assess their understanding?
- How can I help them to evaluate their own thinking?
- Should I take time out for questions? How much time?
- Which questions would best be handled individually outside of class?
- Is this a good time to begin a class discussion?

Madeline Hunter (1982) notes the importance of these decisions as they affect student learning. In her book, *Mastery Teaching*, she draws upon concepts defined through research to offer a number of ideas and techniques which you can employ to enhance your own effectiveness. Although there is little which is radically new here, the simplicity of these "elements of effective instruction" does provide a common language for teaching across various disciplines. As such, the Hunter model can also serve as a framework for planning, providing a handy checklist as you think through everything involved with teaching and learning.

> I like to cycle through these concepts and practices while completing an instructional map. Invariably, I plan too much — too much content and too many activities. I find that the checklist is a good reminder of the things I need to consider, especially if I want to promote a deeper understanding among students. Inevitably, I find it quite easy to cut back if I have prepared too much; moreover, the additional ideas often prove useful when students drift off during lecture or some activity has fallen flat and I need to make a change.
>
> *Bill Timpson*

On the top of any checklist on instruction will always be your understanding of your own goals for content and learning: what you want to get across given your current environment and resources. Any ideas and suggestions you find appealing in this book can (and should) be tailored to your needs and those of your students. Whether during planning, delivery, or review, every teacher faces countless and critical choices. To the extent that you can become a more active and conscious decision-maker, you will energize and improve your teaching while enhancing student success.

Teaching Roles

"Effective teaching" is not a set of generalizable techniques or tricks which can be easily taught just through the listing of "effective elements": it is crucial that you be conscious of what you want to accomplish, and then decide what role(s) you need to perform for your students. The skills that underlie an engaging biology lecture are different from those which help you define the structure of a course, direct your teaching assistants, set grading standards, or provide overall course management. You employ still other skills when meeting with students during office hours, when advising undergraduate majors, or when joining students for informal conversations. In *Teaching Tips* (1990), McKeachie cites six roles that college teachers play:

1. The teacher as *expert* transmits information to students utilizing organizational, presentational, speaking, and listening skills.

2. The teacher as *formal authority* determines objectives and the means for achieving them by defining structure and standards of excellence and by assessing student performance.

3. The teacher as *socializing agent* is the gatekeeper who helps students determine their career paths by clarifying the demands and the rewards of a particular field.

4. The teacher as *facilitator* employs interpersonal skills to help students pursue goals they have determined for themselves.

5. The teacher as *ego* ideally inspires students by modeling personal commitment to a particular discipline and by communicating what makes it exciting.

6. The teacher as *person* enters into mutually validating relationships with students by moving beyond all the other roles he or she plays to reveal personal warmth and trustworthiness.

Goals and Objectives

Once you have clarified your instructional goals, you can specify what you will do — and when, how, etc. — and what you expect your students to learn. These days, with the information base expanding with each year, you may think it impossible to see much beyond basic course coverage. You're not alone. Most teachers in higher education feel pressed for time in class. Clarifying your goals and objectives, however, may open you up to possibilities beyond coverage, where you may want to cut back on surface learning (e.g., listening and repeating) and go for a deeper understanding (e.g., an ability to apply certain concepts).

A few simple goal-related questions may help heighten your awareness of instructional dynamics and the quality of classroom interactions:

- What do you want to gain from teaching this course?
- What do you want your students to be able to do after completing this course? Or this class? Or this assignment?

It is important to note that teaching and learning goals, though related, are not identical, and it is often useful to consider them separately. In assigning a cooperative group project, for example, you may want to assess students' understanding along the way, observe their interactions and serve as both facilitator and resource for the groups. These are *teaching goals.* At the same time, you may want the students to gain experience with a cooperative research project and to improve their interpersonal and communication skills along with mastering the subject matter of the course. These are *learning goals.*

Once you have resolved what you want from your students, you can then consider how best to facilitate their learning. Here, your familiarity with a range of instructional techniques will be useful. In the case of a mid-level foreign language class, for instance, some students will be less well-prepared than others as the term begins. However, it is quite common for an instructor to move straight through required material and place full responsibility for mastery on the shoulders of students, whatever their level of prior preparation. If, instead, the teacher pauses to consider ways to reach the underprepared students early on, the potential for greater student learning increases, while the casualty rate (failures, attrition) drops. For instance, the instructor might turn to the principles of mastery learning (see chapter 8), which emphasizes student success through a step-by-step sequencing of instruction paired with frequent assessment and feedback.

In *The University Teacher as Artist,* Axelrod (1973, 19) points to the teacher, the learner, and the subject matter as the three central and ubiquitous variables of any instructional setting. As a teacher you can choose to emphasize any one of these elements. A presentation is instructor-centered to the extent that you focus on effective delivery. A student-centered approach might include student presentations or small group assignments in class. When subject matter is your concern, you would focus on coverage. To Axelrod's three variables James Wilkinson (1982) adds teaching format, pointing out that learning need not be limited to the classroom.

Once you have clarified the learning objectives you want for students, you can structure your lessons, assignments, and exams accordingly. Students typically value this degree of course integration where expectations are clear and consistent with what happens in and out of class. If you want to state your goals in terms of student performance from knowledge, comprehension, and application to analysis, synthesis, and evaluation, then Benjamin Bloom's seminal work, *Taxonomy of Educational Objectives* (1956), is a helpful reference for teachers at all levels. Norman Gronlund (1985, 33) focuses on objectives as intended learning outcomes in *How to Write and Use Instructional Objectives.* To achieve greater precision in stating objectives, *Principles of Instructional Design* by Gagné, Briggs, and Wager (1988) is also a fine resource.

Readiness

There is no substitute for the enthusiasm and energy that you bring to teaching. Students at all levels rate these qualities highly (see Eble 1994; Lowman 1995, 16); they know when you care about your subject matter and about their learning. In order to be at your best, you will want to prepare yourself physically and emotionally as well as mentally before entering class. Just as actors, dancers, and athletes take time to warm up, so can you put other duties aside for a few moments before teaching. Warm-ups may include meditation, quiet review of the events of the preceding class or of plans for the upcoming class. If the class is large, you may want to include vocal warm-ups which emphasize

> Writing teacher Virginia Draper begins one faculty seminar on teaching by asking everyone in attendance to spend five minutes writing about photosynthesis. After much stalling and embarrassment, especially by those who feel they know little about the topic, everyone writes something down, and Draper has made her point in a way that gets everyone's attention: even when students feel that they have little to say, they can be asked to write what they know or don't know. Once they have done this, you as a teacher have some valuable clues about their readiness for learning.

> Mathematician Ken Klopfenstein has experimented with a cooperative learning component to his course on linear algebra, where students often spend the first twenty minutes of class reviewing homework. Along with getting high levels of student engagement, this process serves as a terrific warm-up for students, quickly pulling them into active roles within small groups, reviewing material from earlier lessons and using the language of mathematics. When Klopfenstein then starts his lecture, a fertile groundwork has already been laid.

projection and clear enunciation. If the material to be presented is complex and challenging, you may want to review the conceptual framework which holds everything together. Looking over student names is also a good idea. Depending on the time in the semester, you may be able to anticipate certain student behaviors. If students are facing an upcoming exam, for instance, they may be feeling anxious, and appreciate some empathy and guidelines for study from you.

Just as you must be ready to teach, so must students be ready to learn. Before class begins, you may find it useful to think through certain questions:

- What knowledge have students demonstrated?
- Do they need certain skills?
- How does the new material relate to what has come before?
- How might a review help them assimilate the new material?
- Have they done the readings or assignments for that day?
- What can encourage their preparation for class?
- What else can maximize learning?

Learning Styles

There is wide variability in the ways students learn best. For example, depending on which of their senses predominates in processing new information, you can describe individuals as primarily visual, auditory, or kinesthetic learners. In other words, some students learn best through reading, others through hearing the new information spoken, and others through writing; many combine two or more of these approaches. The same goes for teaching: which modes do you favor? Do you need to rethink these modes to make your approach more accessible to a wider range of students? By considering learning style differences and designing instruction to reach students in a variety of ways, you increase the odds of student success and, ultimately, your own satisfaction.

Whatever the class format, student learning styles and preferences make for a complex and highly interactive mix of factors which can affect both student success and your own efficiency. In addition to the broad differences described above, some students will prefer to engage actively in class while others are quietly thoughtful. Some are impulsive while others tend to be more systematic. Some can sit comfortably and concentrate for hours while others need regular breaks. In addition, you can learn a great deal about your students simply by observing their behavior in class. Finally, because time in class is limited, you may want to address the variety of student preferences you face by varying the modes of presentation and types of assignments you make.

Students are frequently unaware of their own styles and preferences; there are, however, a number of self-assessment tests available, such as the Meyer-Briggs, which helps individuals determine how they learn best. Spanish teacher Maria Morris administers the Meyer- Briggs Type Indicator Test to her students at the be- ginning of each course both for her own information and theirs. Because she knows her own learning style to be "global/impulsive," she is aware that she needs to be sensitive to those with a different, more deliberate approach. She also hopes to improve learning generally by making students more aware of their own learning styles and preferences.

Reaching All Students

Sensitivity to the diversity among students may lead you to explore new ways to reach all students effectively. A teacher who demonstrates openness to individual differences — whether physical, emotional, or intellectual — can contribute to a more positive classroom climate and, in turn, to increased student success. By empathizing with all students, by seeking ways to involve and motivate everyone, and by maintaining a classroom where students feel able to take risks, you can create the kind of atmosphere which is more conducive to learning.

Teaching students from widely different backgrounds and with differing abilities is not easy. For those who are struggling, those who do poorly on a particular exam or assignment, you can offer remedial activities which provide a chance to catch up before they fall too far behind. Whenever a significant number of students demonstrates a lack of understanding, you need to ask yourself if it is really worthwhile moving ahead. At the other end of the spectrum, you may need to offer enrichment activities to students who quickly demonstrate their command of the material. Also remember that a classroom has a tendency to become a three-ring circus as you continue to address the group in the middle to the exclusion of either end.

Engaged Learning

Consider the entire class period as your allotted time. Now subtract the time required to get started (taking roll, making announcements), the time spent responding to unanticipated interruptions (equipment failure, comings and goings), and the time lost at the end (students preparing to leave): what remains is your instructional time. From that, subtract the time when students are distracted or bored. What is left over is *engaged time*, when students are attentive and involved in learning. If you then subtract those times when students feel overwhelmed or discouraged, you are left with an even smaller period when students actually experience success in learning.

Using this model, you can measure your effectiveness on any given day by the degree of engagement you are getting as well as the amount of success students experience. Maximizing engaged time can be somewhat of an art, though. Providing for variety and active student involvement can take time, but it also may produce a greater degree of engagement. Learning how to budget time effectively is a skill which you will develop with practice, awareness, and feedback.

There are general guidelines, however, that nearly everyone can agree on. A good lecturer tells the class what he is going to tell them, tells them what he wants to tell them, and then tells them what he has just told them, Joseph Lowman (1995) declares in *Mastering the Techniques of Teaching*. Preview and review take time, but they can also help establish a valuable context for learning. A preview can clarify objectives, focus student attention or prepare students for a subsequent class. An outline in a corner of the board can permit everyone to track a lecture as it progresses. Similarly, a review can summarize recent material and support new learning.

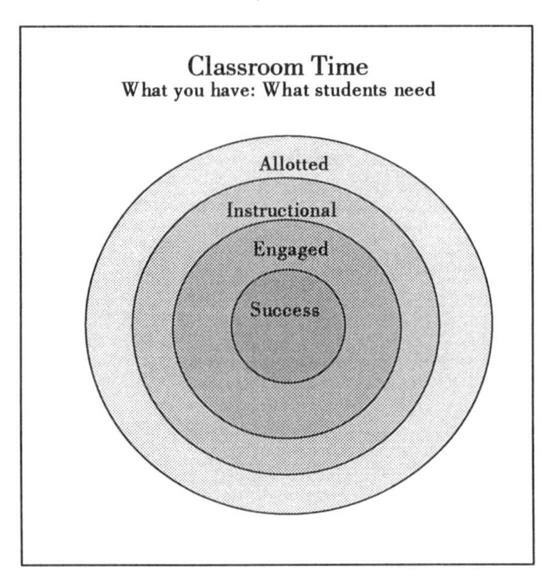

The Conceptual Overview

Whenever you want to reinforce the direction of a course, lecture, lab, or discussion, a *conceptual overview* can be effective. By articulating the concepts and principles that provide the context for a body of ideas, you can help students make more sense out of material, enabling them to process complex information more effectively and to improve their long-term recall. Because the mind is limited in its capacity to remember discrete bits of information (e.g., Miller 1956, 81-97), students need organization and hierarchical categories to structure and support memory. The value of the conceptual overview lies in providing this assistance to the student.

More than a mere description of activities to follow, more than a schedule of readings and assignments, more than a list of instructional objectives, the conceptual overview incorporates central ideas or theories that help explain and organize the facts and information to be learned. In essence, it provides a superstructure for a course, a unit, or a lesson. For example, consider the concepts that might figure in a discussion of Columbus' arrival in the Americas. If the language of *discovery* is used, the mind will organize subsequent information within a category about *new things*. Certainly Columbus and the Europeans learned something new through these explorations, but from the perspective of the native populations, the language of *invasion* or *colonization* may ring much more true. In the mind of the student, a varied vocabulary will involve a variety of cognitive categories, stimulating different thinking and learning patterns.

By developing a conceptual overview, you provide the broad frame-work into which subsequent information can fit. Here you can work with ideas similar or analogous to what students already know, as well as relevant examples and non-examples. You can also include unfamiliar terminology or the specialized vocabulary particular to a discipline. David Ausubel (1963, 50) calls this technique the "advance organizer." His research demonstrates how much more robust is the memory for concepts and principles when compared to the recall of facts and details. Bybee and Sund (1982) point out that the conceptual overview fosters the integration of new information into existing ways of thinking and leads to change of notions which are wrong or limited.

Once you decide about the material you want to require in a course, you can develop a thoughtfully paced schedule of presentations and activities which anticipates the beginning, the middle, and the end of the term. Nash (1984, 70-71) emphasizes the importance of such a comprehensive view.

By designing a course in its entirety, you can clarify your own purposes and direction while offering students a coherent framework for their studies.

Effective Presentations

Your students' ability to recall what you presented in class is enhanced by your own attention to factors like organization, clarity, and pacing. A multi-modal focus can help you address different learning styles. Your vocal skill in pronunciation, enunciation, projection, and timing can contribute to student understanding, interest, and learning. You can improve upon any of these skills over the course of your teaching career: all you need is the motivation. For example, videotaping yourself during a class can be a very enlightening mechanism for feedback, once you get past your own stage fright. A companion volume to this book, *Teaching and Performing: Ideas for Energizing Your Class,* by Timpson et al. (1996) describes in detail the benefits when teachers can draw ideas and techniques from performers.

Eddy is a graduate student and teaching assistant. Below he summarizes his experiences as a student in a class that he found dull, routine, and uninspiring:

> This quarter I am taking a course with someone whose teaching style I really don't like. While there is no doubt that he is quite knowledgeable about the material, he is dry and boring and plods through the 105-minute lecture in a monotone and without a break. He has given out two very intensive homework assignments, and has taken a very long time to return them. There has been very little discussion of where this stuff fits into a larger picture. He 'digressed' once into a discussion of the place of this material in the field as a whole, and it was great — the only time I enjoyed the class!
>
> It is clear that teaching style affects not only how well I learn the material during the lecture, but also my interest level. The material in this class is closely related to a previous class for which my evaluation read, 'Eddy did an outstanding job relative to a group of excellent students.' This suggests to me that I am quite able to work with this particular material, and yet in this class there is a question (in my mind, at least) as to whether I will even pass.

> I also don't get the sense that he has much interest in hearing our responses to the class, and therefore I haven't talked to him about the material or my problems with the way it has been presented. This is unusual for me, as I am generally very involved in my education.

Quite probably, Eddy's teacher had no idea that his student felt this way. If lines of communication had been kept open, and the teacher had paid closer attention to his habits of teaching, chances are he would not have lost this bright and motivated student. Effective instruction should be varied. You can pay attention to the rhythms of a class and consider changes as needed. Something as simple as the use of different colored chalk can improve student understanding of complicated graphs. The overhead projector, slides, videotape, or film can also add valued variety.

Monitoring Understanding

If we accept Wilkinson's description of teaching as a "structured dialogue," the unidirectional lecture diminishes in value. For a dialogue to take place, students must respond in some way to the material that you present. Since you cannot assume complete comprehension on the part of students, checking for understanding is one way to solicit feedback and to engage students in some dialogue, even if their response is as simple as a raised hand. This type of polling is a quick way to determine whether students have understood a certain point or agree with a particular answer. When you pose a question, however, be sure to wait long enough for students to think and articulate a meaningful response. The minute quiz can also be useful for providing immediate feedback for you and your students. Here, you ask students to take out a piece of paper and answer a particular question relating to the material just presented. After a few moments, they

> Mathematician Ed Landesman checks for understanding regularly in his introductory calculus class of 80 students by asking "Get it?" If enough students do not respond with a loud choral "Got it!" Landesman stops, smiles, and asks the question again. It's good-natured and fun, and it helps keep everyone alert. "C'mon," Landesman reminds his students, "I need to hear you. Are you with me? Did you get it?" He thanks them when they respond. If there is genuine confusion, he retraces his steps and addresses whatever problem arises. The beauty of this approach is that Landesman seldom gets so far ahead that students are confused for long. His pace is fast, and the class is highly interactive. In view of the number of students enrolled, it is a remarkable display of ongoing checks for understanding which promotes high student engagement, especially important in a course like this where the material is so challenging.

will be much more prepared to share their responses in pairs or in a large group.

You should also beware of two frequently used but usually ineffective techniques for checking understanding. The first is the classic group question, "Are there any questions?" to which students may be reluctant to reply publicly. The second is the use of the rhetorical "Right?" at intervals throughout a lecture without any other substantive probing.

Physicist Peter Scott models the thinking required to connect mathematical formulas with concrete applications when he presents the effect on a liquid soap solution of two wire rings as they are slowly pulled apart. The demonstration is a rich, resourceful way to lead students through a series of equations to determine the point at which the soap film would burst. By returning to the demonstration several times and relating it to the numbers and formulae on the board, Scott is able to ensure broad understanding of a difficult concept.

Modeling Expectations

To demonstrate the behaviors that you want your students to imitate, and to clarify what you expect of them, you may want to model particular thought processes, problem-solving strategies, laboratory procedures, report writing, public speaking, group work, or any number of other activities. Modeling allows students to see exactly how you want a particular problem attacked or an assignment completed. Once you have done this, students will profit from practicing under your guidance. Following a monitored practice, they can generally complete an assignment more easily on their own.

Closure

Because teachers often feel pressed to cover a prescribed amount of material during class time, the conclusion of a lecture may be hurried or even overlooked. It is often important to take a few minutes at the end of a class to summarize your ideas, relating them to what will be presented next or emphasizing their place within the total conceptual framework of the course. If the class is discussion-based, your synthesis of student contributions can serve to acknowledge the opinions which were expressed and how these relate to the topics, readings, and conclusions at hand. Your recapitulation of important points can also help everyone better assimilate the information presented, especially those students who may have tuned out briefly during class. Remarks about the material just presented or future readings and lectures can also help to stimulate thinking in anticipation of what will follow.

Finally, to gain the most from the teaching experience, you may wish to set aside a short period of time upon leaving class to wind down and evaluate what has just concluded, first, as a distinct teaching experience, and second, within the context of the entire course:

- Were intended objectives met?
- What worked well?
- What could use improvement?

Making a habit of this kind of reflection and analysis will usually help you increase your effectiveness.

EXERCISES

1. Read through this chapter prior to meeting your class; look for opportunities to apply one or two new ideas.

2. As you attend a lecture, think about the ideas in this chapter and pay attention to how the speaker applies different ones in the course of the presentation. How do they contribute to its effectiveness? How might the talk be improved?

3. Consider a recent lesson which did not go as well as you would have liked. What might have changed that outcome and improved the class?

4. Try pairing up with a friend and observing one another's classes. Explore some new teaching concepts and ask your partner to help you evaluate their effectiveness.

CORE CONCEPTS

Teaching goals and objectives

Readiness to teach

Readiness to learn

Learning styles

Engaged learning

Preview and review

Engaging presentations

Closure

CHAPTER FIVE

Lecture and Discussion

Effective lecturers combine the talents of scholar, writer, producer, comedian, showman, and teacher in ways that contribute to student learning. Nevertheless, it is also true that few college professors combine these talents in optimal ways and that even the best lecturers are not always in top form.

Wilbert McKeachie
Teaching Tips

The student who learns in discussion sees learning as it really goes: fitfully, haltingly, speedily with one set of things, stumblingly with another, now following logical pathways, now connecting at unlikely points. The pursuit of truth is ... a game that gives room for error, scope for the imagination, and many different rewards and satisfactions.

Kenneth E. Eble
The Craft of Teaching

Discussion vs. Lecture

The two quotes above illustrate two basics facts about lecture and discussion as teaching formats. As McKeachie points out, the success of the lecture is dependent upon the skills and preparation of the teacher: you can tailor a lecture to your precise specifications, and to the exact needs of your students, and have a sure-fire plan for academic success; but all that beautiful preparation may be compromised if you wake up out of sorts one day or misplace your notes, if you get waylaid at the last minute by an urgent phone call, or wiped out emotionally by an earlier and unproductive meeting, looming deadlines, or the piles of work which greet you upon entering your office. On the other hand, Eble reminds us that a discussion — which can help propel students toward greater insight and a deeper understanding — is frequently a messy and meandering form of education. In this chapter, we'll look at both of these approaches, examine their pros and cons, and offer what we hope will be some useful and fresh perspectives.

There is good reason why these two distinct approaches to instruction have endured in higher education. Each meets a particular need: one brings instructor expertise to novices in an efficient format; the other provides an opportunity for students to articulate and rethink their ideas within an interactive public arena. Both of these needs are central to the purposes of education — learning, practice, reflection, and reevaluation — and if you are clear about your goals and objectives, you and your students can take advantage of each, perhaps even alternating between them in one way or another. Obviously, the constraints of enrollments and classroom layout will play a role here.

Whenever you need to present essential information or ideas, whenever you want to model a way to solve a particular problem or demonstrate some effect, that is the time to lecture — when you need to explain new material, report the most recent experimental results, or offer concrete examples. Once you put these raw materials out into the class, however, you may want to shift to a less rigid discussion format, where students can then wrestle with this information, where they have the opportunity to hear each other's ideas and reassess their own thinking. The active engagement students experience during a discussion contrasts with their more receptive and reflective behavior during a lecture. In short, neither form is "right" for all times and all places; as essential elements lying on opposite ends of an educational continuum, lecture and discussion complement one another and — with creativity, experimentation, and initiative on your part — can be adapted effectively in a wide range of teaching situations.

The Lecture

With the weight of tradition on its side, the lecture endures as the primary instructional vehicle for higher education because it has the potential to challenge and inspire, because it can be perfectly tailored to a teacher's style and beliefs, and because, from a purely pragmatic perspective, it is an efficient way to present material to large numbers of students. Although new instructors rarely receive any formal training in teaching and learning, most have experienced countless hours of lecturing in the course of their own education. Doubtless the quality of these lectures varied widely as a function of a number of factors — including the knowledge, skill, preparation, and enthusiasm of the presenters. So, too, will their own lectures vary in effectiveness. However, research on instructional improvement clearly indicates that teachers can do a great deal to enhance the quality of their presentations. While everyone brings unique characteristics and experiences to the challenges of teaching, the potential to become an effective lecturer lies primarily within your own personal commitment.

What, then, constitutes a good lecture? While there is no simple answer to that question, a number of people — teaching assistants, students, and you yourself — should have a voice in the matter. Among the various factors which you might consider in preparing to lecture, the most important must be student learning: if you make a brilliant presentation that is beyond the understanding of many of the students in attendance, can you be judged effective? A good lecturer will both tailor a presentation to a particular audience and then deliver it well. The following discussion briefly addresses some of the factors that can help you extract the most from your lectures.

Self-Awareness

Good speakers typically have a great deal of self-awareness: they can monitor themselves as they lecture, noticing volume, enunciation, pacing, gestures, and movements. This ability to pay attention to both speech content and delivery is an acquired ability which can help you respond to even the most subtle of factors in your environment. In developing such a "split consciousness," actors learn to monitor their own performance, what the other actors on stage are doing as well as the reactions of the audience. In similar manner, effective teachers commonly develop a split consciousness that allows them to be sensitive to any number of variables in class. As you listen to one student speaking, for example, you can also keep track of who else wants to speak, where the discussion is heading, how much time has elapsed, how much time is left, etc. Your ability to do all this develops naturally over time with experience, practice, feedback, and reflection.

The notion of split consciousness may indeed be at the heart of truly effective teaching: no matter what the format — be it a 250-person lecture or a small group discussion — what goes on in class requires good communication. At any point in time you can get information and impressions from students about their experience, and what and how they are learning. This information may be direct, as in "We don't get it," or it may be much more subtle: a bewildered expression on someone's face, boredom or excitement, laughter. Excessive movement or restlessness, furious note-taking, doodling, sleeping, chatting, or reading the campus paper — all of these convey messages about the progress of the class.

If you pay attention to these kinds of data — some are impossible to ignore — you can increase your chances of keeping students engaged and involved. On one level, you can simply ask students — before or after class, in a formal face-to-face meeting during class time or informally during office hours — how the course is working for them, how it isn't, what recommendations they might have, etc. When you are willing to go beyond course coverage and accept responsibility for assessing student reactions and needs, your teaching will become more dynamic and responsive. To the extent that you gauge your own effectiveness on the basis of student learning, then the value of responding to their needs becomes obvious.

Preparation

While there is no substitute for preparation for a lecture, neither is there a simple formula that can assure complete success. When constructing a new course, you may invest a great deal of time in developing a bibliography and planning a series of topics, assignments, and related activities. When revising an old course, you should reconsider all of these elements, perhaps adding new ideas and references to keep the course fresh. Consider as well the influence of your own personal enthusiasm about the material: if you continue to use the same notes year after year after year, you may look (or be) bored, and your students will react accordingly. It could be well worth the time and effort to revise sections so that you can retain your own engagement with the material. Students at all levels value enthusiasm in their teachers: to the extent that the freshness of lecture material affects your own attitude during preparation, the extra time required to introduce new material may be a wonderful investment that pays handsome dividends.

It is the rare presenter who can deliver material well simply by reading to the audience. If a lecture is to be delivered exactly as written, it may be better to duplicate and distribute the information, dismiss class, and let students decide when and how to study. On the other hand, an oral presentation can be kept lively by changing the pace or emphasis, or by including planned activities. You can always add something spontaneous as opportunities arise. You can also enhance your presentations with rehearsal; a brief review of your notes will free you from bondage to them. By speaking from abbreviated notes and emphasizing key concepts, you can stay more focused on central points while making regular eye contact with students — acknowledging raised hands, noticing reactions — and adjust your presentation accordingly.

In addition to preparing the material for a lecture, it can be just as important for you to prepare yourself emotionally and physically. Stage performers invariably take time before the curtain is raised to warm up and "get into character." Inasmuch as you are a public speaker when lecturing, you should also do what is necessary to get into character. Stretching, meditating, or quietly reviewing notes or names can help.

Because lecturing requires projection, clear enunciation, and vocal variety, it is also important to warm up the voice before starting to teach. Your preparation here can be as simple as a few minutes of humming or singing on the way to class. Such a warm-up can help focus your energy and assist with the emotional preparation you may need, especially for performing in front of large numbers of students. Once class begins, you may also want to warm up your "audience." For example, you can help prepare students for class by resolving certain questions before beginning to lecture, by reminding the class of what was covered in a previous session, by describing the conceptual framework for that day's material and by previewing your goals and learning objectives.

Maintaining an awareness of self is essential for successful lecturing. Before class ever begins, you will need to judge when you have prepared enough, and when it is time to warm up physically and emotionally. Once class begins, you will "watch" yourself while you are teaching, making adjustments as necessary. It may be important, for example, to resist the temptation to answer your own questions; make sure you wait and let students have an opportunity to get involved. You may need to fight a tendency to remain stationary behind the lectern, and learn to move toward those with questions, to the board when you need to write out a name, or across the front as a way to add variety and energy to the class. Like actors, you cannot allow yourself to get so lost in your role — here as content expert — bound and determined to cover everything planned, that you lose your audience.

Organization

The organization of lectures can help determine the ease with which students follow your thinking and learn new material. For example, you could focus more on a few central concepts and then use the time available to fill in some details. As experts, many postsecondary teachers are quick to move into extensive details, digressions, subtleties, and complexities without giving adequate emphasis to the conceptual overview which students — especially those who are unfamiliar with the material — usually require. While the lecture is an effective format, don't overestimate the amount of material that can be covered in any one class session. It may help you to think of your lecture as a conceptual framework for the course, rather than merely as a source of information — it is an intellectual foundation which will underlay student learning later on.

Teachers and students alike can also benefit from a clear statement of goals and objectives. Although they are sometimes difficult to express, a list of learning objectives can help clarify just what students should learn by the end of a lecture or by the end of a course. Students frequently comment on the importance of understanding what was expected of them in their end-of-course evaluations.

Expectations of Students

Whereas much new thinking about instruction emphasizes the active and constructivist learning which students can achieve in small groups in particular, you can also have an impact with up-to-date, well-organized lectures. Here students must exercise a kind of self-discipline which permits them to sit quietly and absorb material for extended periods of time. They need to be simultaneously attentive and reflective, noting questions as they listen. You can help students make the most of the time spent in a lecture by clearly explaining what you intend to cover and what you expect them to retain from a particular presentation. You can encourage them to ask questions; if some students are afraid to speak up in class, you can plan for periodic opportunities where you ask them to discuss a question with a classmate. By then polling the class, you can then quickly discover what they still don't know. You can also help students form study groups for support and assistance outside of class.

Engagement

Critical to the success of any lecture is *engagement*, or the degree to which students are intellectually immersed, emotionally involved, and attentive. While individual engagement is difficult to measure precisely, there are clear outward indications that disengagement has occurred. When chatting starts, when heads go down for naps, when newspapers appear, or when eyes simply glaze over, it is clear that students can no longer concentrate fully on the lecture.

Knowing that student attention spans have their limits, you can intervene to keep everyone focused: surveys, questions, special assignments, group activities, or an occasional digression can help break the routine in class. The time invested should prove worthwhile if students are then able to sustain a higher level of attention for the class time which remains. A word of caution, however: you should announce any digressions as such. If you don't, it may confuse your students — especially the beginners, who are often unable to distinguish between the bedrock subject matter and the digressive discussion.

The quality of instructional time is related to the degree of student engagement during any class period. You should try to handle tasks such as taking roll or handing out papers as efficiently as possible so as to maximize the time which remains. You can measure the quality of time you get in your class by asking someone — a colleague, a teaching assistant, or a member of the class — to keep track of the way time is used on a particular day or

> Both Bettina Aptheker (Women's Studies) and Tracy Larrabee (Computer and Information Sciences) use occasional digressions to keep their classes engaged. Each year Aptheker teaches Introduction to Feminism to a class of some six hundred students. When she senses that they are drifting off and need a change of pace, she often shifts and tells a relevant story. Because stories relating human experiences and feelings are real, often dramatic, funny or quite personal, they provide a compelling contrast to more abstract, theoretical, or intellectual material. Furthermore, students will often remember the specifics of stories and therein have cues for getting to the underlying principles.
>
> Larrabee will occasionally interject a planned digression into a lecture in order to convey "extraneous" material she considers important for students. It is the strength of her own convictions which helps her step outside the strict confines of the course curriculum and engage students with controversial or troubling issues. For example, to encourage the women and raise important issues of equity she will briefly describe her own experiences as one of the only women at Cal Tech. She will also take a few minutes to tell the story of Alan Turing, one of the pioneers of computer science, who was assassinated by the British Secret Service because he was not willing to hide his gay lifestyle.

Mathematician Ken Klopfenstein has redesigned a linear algebra class around a cooperative learning structure. When he has a question he wants answered, he will often use his calculator to assure a random selection of one of the groups to offer a response. With each of the twelve groups assigned a Greek letter and each individual member given one of the letters A through D, Klopfenstein then merely enters a particular function to identify a group and individual. This seems to help keep everyone alert. It's fun to see who the calculator will choose.

series of days. By subtracting the amount of time spent on announcements, handouts, and other interruptions from the total time allocated for the class, you can begin to get a better sense of the instructional time at your disposal. Of that amount only a portion can be considered engaged time, for students occasionally drop their concentration, become distracted, or lose the thread of your lecture. If you can learn to track the time you really have to work with, you will enhance your effectiveness considerably and facilitate more learning.

Group Focus

If you have ever hinted broadly that a certain topic or problem-type might well appear on a future exam and suddenly found your students much more attentive, then you have a feel for what is meant by *group focus*. Essentially, it is your own awareness of group engagement, what factors or strategies can help you pull everyone into the lecture or discussion, as well as those dynamics which make it easier for students to drift off. Group focus is another skill in your *metateaching* (chapter 9) repertoire, permitting you to interact with individual students while remaining quite conscious of the responses from the rest of the class and what, if anything, you could do to involve them.

Learning how to focus an entire class is very useful, and you can do it in many ways. Sometimes, your threat to call on students randomly to respond in front of the class as a whole is enough to cause their adrenalin to pump in anticipation. You can use your class roll. You can also survey students about their opinions and then call for a show of hands indicating who agrees, who does not and who may be undecided. Forcing the issue requires everyone to vote, to think about the question and take a stand.

However you manage it, the key here is to split your consciousness in such a way that you can proceed with your lecture or discussion while staying alert to opportunities which let you engage everyone more directly. Classroom entropy — that tendency for students to devolve into passivity and let others, yourself included, do all the work — can take over quite quickly. As much as you can, use material, topics, and strategies which energize and activate students. When their attention does flag, look for a change of pace — a short writing assignment, a chance for students to briefly discuss their responses in small groups — or pose a question to the class as a whole.

Assessing Readiness and Understanding

Just as your sensitivity to class engagement can help you motivate and challenge students, so too can you facilitate learning by knowing something about the academic backgrounds of your students — the knowledge and skills they bring to class, what they have understood from previous lectures, their feelings about participation, their abilities to communicate effectively and work cooperatively. To determine initial levels of readiness, you can administer a diagnostic test or short quiz at the beginning of a course, or use occasional assessments thereafter — writing assignments in and out of class, responses to questions, group projects, journals. For example, by asking for a show of hands to indicate how many students understand, how many do not, or how many might have a question about some detail, you can quickly determine whether to move ahead with your presentation. You can obtain more detailed information with a "minute quiz," where you ask all students to write down on a piece of paper the answer to a particular question related to the topic of the lecture. You can then discuss these with the entire class or read them later to help yourself prepare for the next lecture.

> Bettina Aptheker (Women's Studies) points to several factors outside course content which affect learning. For example, she emphasizes the value of silence in any class, pointing out what amazing things can be said during moments of instructor silence, those pauses after key questions or unsettling conclusions. She also pays attention to body language, to the restlessness which may mean a shift of focus, to making the kind of eye contact with students which can help personalize a large class. That's not simple in a class of six hundred, but her alertness to these nuances does make a difference to students.
>
> Mathematician Ken Klopfenstein will stop his lecture when he senses that students in his linear algebra class seem confused: "You look puzzled," he'll say empathetically to a particular student and then wait for a response. Likewise, Sandy Kern (Physics) uses a pause after he makes a point or completes a problem to scan the two hundred fifty or so students in introductory physics for signs of disbelief. Frequently, he'll follow this with a poll — "How many think it's this? How many think it's that? How many think it's something else altogether?" — to ferret out those with enduring misconceptions but too reticent to ask anything in such a big lecture class.

Variety

Supplementing the lecture with other instructional techniques can also ensure better connection between you and your students. By using a discussion format or by assigning small group projects occasionally during class time, you can become acquainted with students on an individual basis and get a better sense of their understanding and needs. When individuals or small groups make presentations before the entire class, you get a chance to see your students from yet another perspective.

Students usually appreciate the variety represented by occasional changes of pace and activity. Some instructors will intentionally structure an activity in the midst of a lecture to provide a needed break in routine. Individual or small group projects can create opportunities for more active student learning. By varying the ways in which you present material, you can reach more students effectively, since individual learning styles or preferences differ from person to person. Kinesthetic learners may do better with concrete, hands-on experiences; visual learners may want to see a written version of what they are listening to; and auditory learners may like to hear as they read. Similarly, some students may learn best when they can articulate new ideas out loud, while others may do best when allowed to think quietly. Some learners can be best described as analytic and others as impulsive. When facing students with varied styles and preferences, you may have your greatest success when you can use a variety of approaches.

Here is a simple example: if you use a word processor to compose your lecture notes, make this material available for distribution in class, via e-mail, or for placement on reserve at the library. The availability of this text will permit students to read and reread lecture material outside of class, leaving them free to listen more attentively during class, perhaps even providing a more engaged audience for the presenter. Also, students who are preparing for exams often appreciate a printed study guide.

Students as Resources

The unhelpful idea that the teacher is the sole source of information and expertise in a class is not only wrong — it translates into more work and drudgery for you. If you use collaborative groups, you already know about the tremendous learning potential when students can work together effectively. Cooperative group work in and out of class seems to benefit most learners. Students can also play an effective role as editors of each other's papers. By offering feedback to their peers on early drafts of writing assignments, students contribute to the improvement of those papers while increasing their own awareness of the writing process. Students can also help write questions for exams. This activity expands the pool of questions you have available and helps students to think about the kinds of questions you might ask on midterms and finals.

Enhancing Retention

A growing body of research has isolated a number of factors which can enhance student retention of lecture material. A high level of student engagement and active participation in learning certainly helps. In addition, students tend to recall information better when lecture material is meaningful or relevant to them: when you make an effort to help them assimilate the material through links or associations to what they already know, when you involve their varied senses, and when you can help them tap their imaginal abilities or create opportunities for hands-on learning, students should experience a much greater engagement with the material.

You may also help promote student success by reserving some class time for discussions about ways to increase retention, especially in first-year classes. Some students may lack basic knowledge of study and test-taking skills. You can tell these students that taking notes during lecture, for example, reproduces information and ideas in written and kinesthetic form. You can also emphasize key concepts, and provide cues to help students organize their notes, as well as their thinking, both during the lecture, and later on, when they need to review their notes.

Bettina Aptheker (Women's Studies) exploits the talents of her students in a different way, and, at the same time, adds diversity and interest to the structure of her course, Introduction to Feminism. She recruits graduates from the Intro course as leaders for discussion sections. These students bring their own experiences, interests, energy, and creativity into the mix of learning options available to those enrolled in the large lecture course. As a result, each section has a different focus. Because the section leaders are all simultaneously enrolled in a seminar that Aptheker runs in parallel to the large lecture class, she can maintain close supervision and support for what happens in the sections. The benefits of this approach are many: discussion sections provide valuable opportunities for more active student learning; section leaders themselves get the kind of teaching assistant's role usually reserved for graduate students; Aptheker gets to work more closely with these section leaders and explore course material in greater depth; and the course as a whole is enriched by the varied teaching talents assembled together.

Attendance

Attendance is often a concern for lecturers, especially when classes are large. Generally speaking, students are more likely to come to a class where they can expect to hear a well-structured and effectively delivered lecture, but even if you're not naturally the most dynamic lecturer, there are a

Historian Loren Crabtree and folklorist Carol Mitchell pass around attendance sheets with severe penalties (lowered grades) for those students who exceed a certain minimum number of absences. Students seem to be quite understanding and accepting of all this even when it may be the early start time which is problematic.

Ken Klopfenstein often begins his course on linear algebra with time for cooperative groups to meet and share their results from the homework assignment. Every student has a responsibility to a group to be an expert on one particular problem for each class period, to present a carefully worded solution. Missing class means a loss of points as well as incurring the disapproval of other group members. Attempting a solution earns some points while making an especially effective presentation accrues even more.

Physicist Sandy Kern, however, weaves a special kind of magic in his large introductory course for non-majors. When pressed to explain their regular attendance, students describe Kern's effectiveness in very glowing terms, noting how his use of examples makes it easier for them to understand difficult abstract material, how his attentiveness to their questions provides the extra measure of time they often need to resolve confusions, how his humor and friendliness help nurture the confidence many need to overcome their fears and misconceptions about the subject. In physics, many fundamental principles are indeed quite nonintuitive and their mastery appears to be a very delicate process indeed.

number of ways to promote attendance. For example, if they know that their presence in class will be reflected in their final grade, they will attend class more regularly. Accordingly, you will have to keep an attendance roster and decide if the extra time and effort is worth it. The best policy we can recommend here is that you try to be clear about this from the first day of class.

Another alternative is the occasional in-class assignment, which can give you direct evidence of who was in attendance. Unannounced quizzes are almost guaranteed to get more students coming to class — and coming better prepared — although the anxiety you engender this way may have a negative impact on classroom climate. Whatever you decide to do, be sure to give your reasons. Students are often quite accepting of a teacher's decisions if they receive a reasoned explanation. For example, you may want to structure your classes around discussions, but if you later discover that the quality of your time in class varies directly with the degree of everyone's attendance and prior preparation, then you need to alter the class structure to ensure uniform participation, and explain to the class what you're doing, and why.

Whether or not you decide to keep track of attendance, you will always want to make class time productive and interesting for students. For example, attendance will tend to rise when students know that you will answer their questions, provide alternative explanations, offer different examples, clarify assignments, or provide some guidance for upcoming exams. Just beginning on time can send a message to students that may increase attendance. Thanking those students who do attend is another form of positive reinforcement that many teachers overlook in their concern about those who are absent. Appealing to students to support their peers when they are presenting projects in class can also promote a positive class climate and thereby increase attendance.

Students also appreciate it when they know that you will be available before and after class for individual questions, or if you regularly reserve a few minutes of class time for questions. When you do respond to questions in class, however, you will want to keep an eye on the needs of the entire class (a group focus) so that a response to one student does not monopolize the time available and bore everyone else. A quick show of hands can help you decide this; you may do better by addressing the issue privately and outside of class.

Discipline

Student behavior during lectures is a topic that few teachers in higher education like to talk about. Nevertheless, problems can and do arise. Large classes have their own special challenges, induced, in part, by anonymity and a lack of direct student-instructor contact. What can be done when some students chat during the lecture and disturb others? What about those who come late or leave early? What about those who act out?

You can simply confront noise or tardiness directly as it occurs, or you may choose to speak privately with those responsible. You may want to consider a hierarchy of potential interventions, thinking first of a subtle "Quiet please" or "Sshhh" but then moving up toward a more direct response to those involved. While you may be able to prevent some problems with a clear articulation of your expectations about student behavior at the beginning of a course, there is no substitute for swift intervention at the time a problem occurs: don't be reluctant to interrupt your lecture to address an offending student — for every student who thinks you are being harsh, there will be dozens who believe you and they are entitled to certain conditions in class.

Questions

As common as questions are in university courses, they can sometimes weaken a lecture, causing digressions and affecting momentum. One idea is to prepare important questions ahead of time and pose them during class, thereby piquing student interest, enhancing engagement, and monitoring understanding. If, however, you reveal the answer before students have had a chance to reflect and formulate their own responses, the question becomes strictly rhetorical and may lose its instructional impact. If this is a concern for you, try the following: When posing these questions, count silently and slowly to five before proceeding; this will ensure a period of time during which students can think through an answer as well as muster the courage to volunteer a response.

It is also important to consider *wait-time* whenever you ask for questions. A short pause communicates your willingness to hear from students, as well as your conviction that even a lecture is in part a two-way communication. In responding to individual inquiries, you should take care to come to your point as clearly and directly as possible. By devoting too much time to a single question, or by feeling that you must address every question, however arcane, you may lose both momentum and your audience.

The Discussion

In contrast to the lecture, discussions provide an environment where students can participate more actively and directly, learning to think by articulating their ideas and hearing from others. Whenever you want students to know how to apply principles, analyze ideas, formulate and solve problems, evaluate positions, or to integrate learning, the discussion is an effective format. As an arena for free and spontaneous interchange of ideas, discussions allow students to express their own thoughts, doubts, and confusions. Vital, stimulating, unpredictable, and sometimes emotional, discussions can challenge both you and your students to pass beyond the level of simple curriculum coverage.

As teacher, you play a number of roles during a discussion — although a few students may be capable enough to perform some of them on occasion as well. As leader of the discussion, your job is to pose critical questions, monitor the time available, maintain a focus on the task at hand, and facilitate interaction among the participants. In comparison to a lecture, the discussion will inevitably have less structure; accordingly, it will be that much more important for you to be alert to group dynamics and your instructional goals, ready to intervene if necessary to get a derailed process back on track.

There are limitations, of course, to the discussion format, and many of these limitations are imposed by the external conditions of the class. The first consideration is *class size*: with a group of about twenty students, the discussion format can be very powerful. It is more difficult in large classes, especially those located in rooms where tables are bolted and you cannot rearrange the seating. For a discussion to succeed, students must be able to hear what others say, and ideally they will be able to see all the other participants as well. You may be able to alleviate some of the problems imposed by large classes if you can divide students into smaller, cooperative groups. Another approach is common in disciplines like law and business, where teachers make regular use of case studies to evoke discussions with even very large classes. Whichever way you proceed, discussions can help you promote a high degree of participation and interject some welcome sparks of spontaneity and variety, all of which can combine to energize students and bolster attendance and preparation.

Discussion and Thought

The primary benefit of classroom discussion is its emphasis on individual thinking skills. When students read quietly or listen to a lecture, a whole range of variables affects the ways they assimilate new information — their previous knowledge of the subject, their personal history, their interest in the material, and their readiness to learn that day. These factors may actually alter the intended message of the writer or the speaker and, consequently, affect how students learn. Bouton and Garth (1983, 75), for example, emphasize the importance for students to speak about notions that they do not fully understand. Indeed, a discussion between you and some of your students can also be an invaluable aid in determining how they are thinking about course material and where confusions might be lurking.

Discussion also provides students with an opportunity to experiment with ideas in the public arena, to test and deepen their understanding, to begin to construct coherent intellectual systems, and to assimilate new ideas. By putting new information into their own words, students can begin to make it their own. In addition to enhancing the development of a range of cognitive skills, discussion provides a wonderful format for the clarification of values. As students formulate and express their thoughts, hear how others respond and what they themselves believe, they get a chance to reflect upon their own learning and reactions.

By noting how various discussions proceed, you can get a feel for the evolution of intellectual and emotional development in the class: in this regard, the social nature of the interaction among students and their teachers in higher education makes discussion a powerful vehicle for

When I begin to prepare a lecture, I like to start with a blank sheet. It is tempting to pull out last year's notes — and sometimes I do — but I also like the challenge of starting fresh, of taking a different tact or introducing new material, pulling on something current, something in the news, perhaps. It's unnerving to start over each time, but I like the creative impetus. I also like the energy (tension, anxiety) which flows from a blank sheet and the requirement to produce something which will engage students and facilitate their learning. When I can find the time and inspiration to start over like this, I do feel better about my responsibilities as a lecturer.

What often happens, however, is that I never start over completely, but borrow from my own perceived "greatest hits," those ideas and activities which seemed to resonate with students in the past. And indeed, this hybrid strategy of beginning anew but referencing what has worked before may be the best recommendation I can offer. It works for me.

When the talk is brand new, I do often feel intimidated at the start of my preparation. Where to begin? How? What to include in the time available? Often I like to work backwards from my goals and objectives for students, what I hope they will learn, to the information and ideas and activities which should then comprise the lecture. This approach helps me stay grounded in the outcomes I want, a way to structure my planning and discipline my delivery, for what good is the best of preparation on my part if there was no learning, no interest, no engagement?

Gauging the time needed is a tough call for me, since I like to involve students frequently and at various levels. Experiment. Reflect. Check in with students. Rehearse ahead of time. Your own skills will evolve with experience, self-reflection, feedback, and your own desire to improve.

When I think about delivery, I shift into a consideration of the various approaches I could use to add variety or promote more active learning. For example, I regularly like to put questions to a vote, to poll those present and try to get everyone to engage enough to take a stand, one way or the other. I also like to have students turn to each other and compare ideas or solutions — a bit of active learning to spice up what is otherwise for students a primarily passive, teacher-directed process. I always try to stay grounded in those factors which would make attendance by students rewarding; i.e., they will learn something; I will be organized, energized, and attentive to their learning; and that I will be do my best to make our time together stimulating for them (and me), challenging and, at times, fun.

I must admit that I do enjoy the performance aspect of the direct teaching process, the opportunity to weave together various ideas and information, to describe my own understanding of an issue or concept. I love to pull from a wide range of sources and explore various subtleties and complexities, raising questions along the way and challenging students to think both deeply and broadly. What a thrill when I can tell a story in a way that really seems to hook my students' interests, or organizes the subject matter in a particularly clear and cogent manner, perhaps tying everything up in an elegant intellectual bow just before the period ends. What a privilege I feel I have with attentive students willing to listen to my take on a topic — having paid my dues teaching for two years at the junior high school level, I am especially appreciative when I don't have to beg, bribe, entertain or intimidate students so they will listen!

I find that I do have to maintain a high level of concentration to lecture well, alert to a number of competing factors at the same time — the content, my own delivery (projection, pacing, use of board or overhead, etc.) student reactions, the time remaining, the choices I have in exploring examples or digressions which might clarify certain concepts, the need for a periodic change of pace. Here the notion of metateaching becomes important for me as I try to watch myself lecture and work my way through all these competing factors. Here is where I would also refer to my instructional map (described in an earlier chapter) as well, where I chart our the major activities and goals.

As for improving, I can offer a number of suggestions which have worked well for me. The first involves open lines of communication with students. I always try to build a climate of trust which then allows students to tell me when something works or when they're confused. Near the middle of each semester I also take the time to hold a classroom meeting where students work through their appreciations and concerns, offering concrete recommendations for improving the class while there is still time to make some changes.

In my research for this book, I sat in on several courses, interviewing students and holding a running conversation with the teachers after each class session. While my colleagues appreciated the feedback, I also learned a ton, taking on what I saw and thinking through applications for my own classes. As an observer I had the luxury of time to watch and listen for student reactions, to think through various ideas without having to manage instruction myself.

Finally, ten years of work with telecourse development has also proved invaluable, giving me regular opportunities to see myself teach over the years — and occasional opportunities to cringe at those truly dorky clothes I used to wear! As important, perhaps, has been the pressure to interface effectively with students at a distance, to sequence my courses carefully. That attention to organization has folded back on to my preparation for teaching on campus.

Bill Timpson

personal growth. Students can learn to listen better to others, to accept differences of opinion, and to respect others regardless of their viewpoints. Lowman (1995) insists that the discussion can enhance your rapport with students as well as bolster their independence and motivation in ways that the lecture by itself cannot.

Engagement

Perhaps the most compelling reason for using discussions is to promote engagement and active student learning. In a discussion, students must shift from a passive and receptive mode to an active and generative one. Participating in a discussion can be a much more demanding task than listening to a lecture: students must be able to analyze what has been said and formulate their own responses to comments and questions. A poorly designed (or poorly guided) discussion, however, will lower student engagement. If, for example, a few students dominate the conversation, others often tune out. Similarly, if the leader goes off on tangents and never achieves any closure, students may lose sight of the bigger picture and become lost and bored. Discussions can also fail if you are impatient, too quick in stating your personal opinion or so committed to one perspective that you deny students the opportunity to draw different conclusions about the material.

Engagement will inevitably increase to the extent that the topic is of interest to those enrolled. You may want to identify issues within your discipline which students genuinely care about, and organize related discussions around them. More often, however, your task is to introduce new topics and material to students and let your own enthusiasm energize your students. Much learning inevitably happens by example, and students will be moved and inspired by your genuine interest. Engagement also increases with your skill at sustaining a group focus. Questions and comments from individual students can always be used to stimulate the entire class.

Organization

Without doubt, the biggest constraint on discussion-based instruction is time: the time it takes to explore a topic with any degree of completeness, the time to evaluate the discussion process itself and consider possible improvements, and the time you need to teach basic communication and participation skills. A successful discussion calls for a serious commitment to planning, facilitation, and evaluation. With less time for traditional content coverage, you need to be clear about the advantages you see in the potential of a discussion to achieve deeper understanding and better critical thinking through more active student participation.

Once you have opted for a discussion format, it is important to consider specific objectives for each session. Because a discussion is more dynamic and unpredictable than a lecture, it is best to de-emphasize content slightly and focus more on the *process* of learning. Kasulis (1984, 40-42) calls for a process plan that specifies *how* material will be discussed. For example, you can decide in advance whether you want the class to engage in controversy or in consensus-building, in free exchange of ideas or systematic analysis, in problem solving, role playing, or classroom meetings (where you periodically assess the effectiveness of the class itself). In any case, it's vital to tell your students about these goals, since a process plan helps everyone to maintain a better focus once the discussion has begun. Later, if you find that the focus is fading amid the variety of ideas and opinions expressed, your plan can provide a ready reference point. At any time, of course, you can decide to adjust, ignore, or even abandon the plan should a better plan emerge spontaneously.

You may wish to compile notes or develop an outline to guide your discussion periods. Many students find it quite helpful to have a list of primary objectives, key concepts, or central questions as either a handout or up on an overhead. This can also serve as a conceptual framework or overview where everyone sees how ideas relate to the core concepts under study. Students can later use such outlines when preparing for an exam or a paper.

You must also think through some practical organizational matters. Will you want students to raise their hands and be recognized before speaking, or can anyone speak at any time? Do you want them to respond to the issue at hand, or can they address any and all issues? Who will moderate? Who will synthesize and summarize? How much time will you reserve for this? Who will monitor the time remaining so that closure is possible? Although many of us routinely run period-long discussions, Lowman (1995) recommends ten to fifteen minutes as the optimal discussion length. When a discussion lasts more than thirty minutes, he maintains, it benefits only a few while frustrating most others.

Once a discussion is underway, you need to maintain your vigilance to keep the class on track. Everyone knows how easy it is for discussions to wander. After specifying the topic and the process for the class meeting again, it's a good idea to reinforce them with an outline on the board or on an overhead projector, thereby providing students auditory and visual cues for staying on task. Sharing this responsibility with students can also be helpful in maximizing participation.

Just as it is a good idea to maintain a clear focus in a discussion, so is it important to move toward closure when the time is right. An effective leader recognizes when most students have had their say and alerts the group when it is time to begin wrapping up the discussion. A summary of major ideas and concepts, either by the group leader or by student participants, can be helpful here. A writing exercise following a discussion can help students reflect on what occurred, consider the impact on their own thinking and what new insights they may have. If you feel you need more time for a particular topic, you can make those plans at the end of class as well.

Participation vs. Answer-Seeking

While your own objective for holding a class discussion may include the nurturing of critical and creative thinking, reality will often crash in on your loftier ideals when students want to know more about the next exam. The success of a discussion may vary greatly depending upon your ability to manage and balance these two — often conflicting — goals. Here you might want to think of a discussion as a class which functions with two focal-points, and you shift between the two as needed. A *convergent* focus would have you guiding students toward certain ideas, for instance, via questions that require specific answers. When appropriate, then, you can help your students converge upon particular conclusions or concepts, as well as understand the underlying logical processes.

The other direction for a discussion would involve a *divergent* focus, where you hope to expand student thinking and engage them actively in the construction of knowledge and understanding. When you decide that it is more important to help students develop their own opinions and convictions than to memorize a collection of facts, then you will want to ask more open-ended questions and solicit personal opinions. These kinds of discussions can challenge students to think more critically and creatively, and often prove to be a great benefit to everyone in the class.

Encouraging Participation

Discussions tend to flow most easily around those who want to participate. Most teachers would like to involve everyone at least occasionally, but it is not always easy to do so. By calling on students who are not volunteering, discussion leaders risk provoking anxiety in those who are shy or reticent.

To overcome a reluctance to join in, Kasulis (1984, 40-42) suggests that instructors distribute study questions, making specific students responsible for certain responses and calling on them as the topics arise during discussion. By allowing students to talk about their ideas in small groups prior to the general discussion, more will feel better prepared to join in later on. Similarly, Segerstrale (1984, 63) recommends assigning short opinion papers or topic papers to form the basis for discussion in class. Brief in-class writing assignments at the beginning of the hour can also help students recall relevant ideas and information from readings or lectures and focus their thoughts for the ensuing discussion.

Dreikurs (1968) has written extensively about problems from the other extreme: students who over-participate, who seek attention or power and interfere with the progress of the course. A gentle request can often help you regain control from a particular student who is monopolizing the discussion: "I'd like to hear from those who have not responded yet." McKeachie (1990) suggests raising the topic of participation in the course of discussion: "Would the class be more effective if participation were more evenly distributed?" He also advocates speaking to such students privately outside of class, and pointing out that, while their input is valuable to the class, they need to exercise some restraint for the benefit of their shyer classmates.

During discussion some individuals may be reluctant to speak candidly for fear of expressing an unusual or unpopular point of view. Inclass writing assignments can be of help here, providing students an outlet for free and private expression of ideas. Once they have thought through their opinions and written them down, students often feel more comfortable sharing with others verbally. Especially in a large class, you can use a "fishbowl" technique, where a small group holds a discussion and others observe and then offer feedback. Although time-consuming, you can use this technique to heighten student consciousness about the interplay of discussion and group dynamics.

Participation Skills

The requirements for effectiveness in a discussion differ from those in a lecture, where you are the central focus for students. The interactive nature of a discussion makes clear enunciation and projection important issues for all participants. Similarly, everyone should be reminded to keep comments brief and to the point, to listen carefully to others, showing respect, acceptance, and empathy. You may find it useful to alert each class to these requirements, asking that all students take responsibility for indicating when they cannot hear, when they would like a comment repeated, or when they feel the discussion has bogged down or gotten off track when they don't feel "heard." Once students gain an understanding of the factors that promote effective discussions, they can also participate actively in recommending changes in format or procedure at the very outset of a discussion.

To really enhance the quality of student participation and subsequent learning, you may want to spend some time educating students about group dynamics and training them in effective communication skills. By taking time early on to develop these social skills, you can promote more effective discussion sessions throughout a course of study. Something as simple as pointing out that a speaker is enunciating unclearly or speaking too softly can make a difference.

Developmentalists like Piaget, Bruner, and Kohlberg have always maintained that students learn best through active engagement with new information. Because discussion calls for public expression of ideas, however, some students may feel uncomfortable taking part. McClelland (1985) points to the fear of failure as a block to participation while Lowman (1995) underlines the importance of positive reinforcement for promoting involvement. You should always be on the lookout for ways to select and emphasize the best parts of student comments in class.

The anxiety students may experience in a discussion can also motivate them to prepare better for class. Developmentalists point to tension as a catalyst for cognitive and affective growth, which challenges students to rethink their positions in the face of disagreement or conflicting evidence. As the teacher, however, you need to be aware of the extent to which this anxiety is healthy stress. Frequently, conflicts regarding gender, background, race, sexual preference, personality, etc., are brought into class, and exert a negative influence upon everyone present. Classroom dynamics are complex, and this complexity increases during a discussion. However, your sensitivity and flexibility, combined with open and honest communications, help overcome impediments while promoting growth.

Assessing Impact

The opinions of all participants are important when evaluating the effectiveness of any discussion, and they may vary widely. Whereas you may have enjoyed the pursuit of a particular idea in all its complexity and detail, students may feel bored or confused. By taking a few moments to discuss what transpired, you and your students can gain a better understanding of needs and expectations: such information and awareness can ensure the success of future discussions.

In any debriefing session, students should have an opportunity to think about what occurred in a constructive way, knowing that you will hear their appreciations as well as offer concrete responses to their concerns and recommendations. You will want to seek agreement with students about how to proceed in the future, but beware of excessive zeal in trying to accommodate everyone, and thereby turning your teaching into a popularity contest. "Entertain me!" is sometimes the unspoken demand of the irresponsible, bored student who resists the personal effort required for learning. You may well have felt pulled at times to keep that student interested; you need to be sensitive to this urge, and learn how to resist it without shutting down the class.

Grading

Whether you are lecturing, discussing, or using some mixture of each, your system of evaluation is always going to be a central concern for students. They will want to know what you will expect and how they will be graded. For obvious reasons, it is important to take time during class to clarify course requirements and grading, to make sure everyone knows what a particular exam is testing, and what the due dates for written assignments are.

Evaluating student participation in discussions can also present problems. For what will you hold students accountable? Will you maintain records of participation? Again, you need to consider the individual class, and make your decision based upon your own teaching style and the nature of the course. Once you have made this decision, make sure that the students are aware of your expectations. If, for instance, you decide to grade participation, you will need to work out a system for doing so impartially and consistently. During a discussion, pay attention to who speaks and what they say. Then spend a few minutes attending to record-keeping immediately after class. In this way, you will be able to justify the grades you give, note critical points, and comment on participation. As you get to know your students better, you will find it easier to recall the most important ideas which arose.

Grading strategies can be exploited for the benefit of the class as a whole in other ways as well. An in-class discussion of an exam or papers can become part of the feedback students receive during the course of the semester. Although you need not feel obliged to deal with individual questions or challenges during class time, you can use this time to remind students of the objectives of the course, and of your expectations for them. Individual concerns can also be resolved within the group as students understand more about their mistakes and how they can improve their performance in the future.

The feedback you provide when exams and assignments are returned helps to ensure student success with subsequent projects. You can also orient students in advance of a test or assignment by providing copies of past exams or papers for the library or copy center, or by including them in course handouts. This approach allows students to get a sense of what you are looking for without having to wait for the first exam or paper to be returned and discussed. If there is only one assigned paper or one mid-term in a course and no opportunity to see previous tests, students have less opportunity to figure out what you want. To prepare students for an exam without using up precious class time, consider holding a review session during office hours.

Inevitably, you will have some "group" complaints with whatever grading system you choose. Accordingly, you need to make provisions for conflicts over grades, and then inform your students. For example, you may want to announce at the beginning of the semester that you will accept written appeals for grade changes, but only when supported by justifications. In addition, you may want to encourage group appeals, where students come together to review an exam, for example, and attempt to reach consensus about issues pertaining to grading inequalities. A great advantage of this sort of process is that students will invariably make a concerted effort to review the exam results and win back some points. And *Surprise!* they learn the material all over again and at a deeper level as they go over their results, consult with the text, and discuss the viability of various appeals. This approach also has the benefit of uncovering bad exam questions, enhancing classroom climate and demonstrating your willingness to admit errors and reevaluate grades.

I love discussions, that is, when the topic is hot and everyone seems engaged, when we are exploring the subtleties of complex issues or working the space between theory and practice. I thrive on the depth and breadth of some of these conversations, the need to pull from a wide range of sources, to see new connections, and to do it all in the moment. But I do get exasperated when discussions don't go well, when students are not engaged, weary, or unwilling to join in. I hate it when someone asks how I will test what happens in the discussions — the ultimate albatross around my teaching neck. The goal is learning, as deep and meaningful as possible. My exams and assignments attempt to assess student understanding, but never as a linear function of everything we do in class.

To maximize my chances for success in a discussion, I first attend to climate — those feelings of trust and safety which can allow for free and open communications. Names are important here, and I put some time and effort into learning who my students are, their majors, interests, concerns. I also want them to know each other's names, to respect everyone's contributions and not just play to me and my approval.

I try to use a circle so that everyone can make eye contact. If the tables are fixed — Arggh, I wonder when campus architects will listen to those who actually teach — I'll move up and down the rows, fielding questions, sparking debates, soliciting reactions, changing my physical proximity to students to prompt engagement, learning, and rethinking. I like the intensity of a spirited discussion, where intellectualism can meet passion and concern in a more holistic forum.

I do worry some about closure, about wrapping everything up in a tidy package, all the various threads and thoughts converging onto some reasonable conclusion. Short of that fantasy, I just try to trust the process, that good things will happen when everyone is actively engaged in something important and that there is much power (and learning) in the resulting synergy.

Metateaching (chapter 9) is as important to a good discussion as to an effective lecture. I always find it a challenge to manage the mix of relevant factors here — the content, student participation, the time remaining, the goals and learnings, my own facilitation, the climate in class. And as with lecturing, I find the instructional map (chapter 9) useful as a reference. At any point I can look over what I had planned and get a quick visual or verbal reminder as a reference.

Bill Timpson

EXERCISES

1. Review a recent lecture you presented in light of this discussion of concepts and effective practices. Note any discrepancies. Could the lecture have been more effective if you had done some things differently?

2. Attend an upcoming lecture with the goal of evaluating its effectiveness.

3. Cycle through these concepts and practices systematically as you prepare future presentations. What changes would you like to experiment with? Focus on one at a time. After a lecture, take some time to reflect on the impact on yourself and your students of any changes that you made.

4. Have one of your lectures videotaped. In viewing the tape, identify ways in which the lecture was effective as well as areas for change or improvement. Then invite a friend to view the video and to perform the same evaluation. Discuss your points of agreement and disagreement.

5. To enhance your professional growth, make a commitment to sit in regularly on lectures presented by others. Take notes about what works and what could be handled differently. Look for ideas and strategies that you could try in one of your classes. Talk to the students to discover what they value and what concerns or recommendations they may have. Share your observations and these student comments with the lecturer. (Note: In chapter 10, we go into some detail about peer coaching and feedback.)

6. Reflect on a group discussion in which you participated recently. What worked and what did not? Would it help to do anything differently next time?

7. Design a discussion around a controversial issue. How will you manage participation?

CORE CONCEPTS

The Lecture

Presenting information

Split consciousness

Preparation for "performance"

Organization

Engagement and group focus

Discipline

The Discussion

Facilitating student thought

Organization vs. spontaneity

Encouraging participation

CHAPTER SIX

Encouraging Creativity and Promoting Discovery

The responsibility for change ... lies with us. We must begin with ourselves, teaching ourselves not to close our minds prematurely to the novel, the surprising, the seemingly radical. This means fighting off the idea-assassins who rush forward to kill any new suggestion on grounds of its impracticality, while defending whatever now exists as practical, no matter how absurd, oppressive, or unworkable it may be.

Alvin Toffler
The Third Wave

A strong tradition of creativity and innovation ought to be the life-blood of higher education. Futurists like Toffler agree that inventiveness will become increasingly crucial to society in years to come as problems arising from an increasingly automated and complex world demand increasingly novel approaches. With research and inquiry built into the heart and soul of the university, the encouragement of creativity should certainly have a place in teaching.

Yet, this is often not the case. Along with the skewing of rewards toward publications and funded grants, the other main culprit may be the need for curriculum coverage. Faculty across the various disciplines typically insist that a certain foundation of knowledge must be laid before students can be expected to think critically or creatively. However, if teachers are preoccupied

Physicist Burt Jones sometimes pauses during a lecture and presents students with data that is largely unexplained. Why, for example, do sun spots vary in intensity and frequency in consistent patterns over eleven-year cycles? The presentation of this problem, and any discussions which follow, can help re-engage students whose attention has drifted. Here, Jones temporarily relinquishes his role as lecturer and becomes instead a facilitator of learning, probing and pushing students to think for themselves, and making a temporary shift in the nature of his relationship with students.

with laying this (ever-expanding) foundation, there is little time or energy left for innovative additions. Compounding this problem is the confusion over "creativity" as an aspect of the curriculum. While the transmission of information is a relatively straightforward objective, the encouragement of creativity is much more elusive. Just what does *creativity* mean for teachers and their students? How can you encourage it, and how can you assess it?

Creativity Described

Most people have an intuitive sense of what creativity is: generally, we think of it as the ability to jump out of established ways of thinking and acting, to experiment with new ideas and methods, to keep careful track of what holds promise, and what is a dead end. This ability to think in new ways is of course a fundamentally personal one, but there are similarities from person to person. From both empirical research and individual testimony, it is possible to sketch a general picture of what the creative process looks like and how it proceeds (e.g., Patrick 1955). For your needs as a teacher, it is possible to present the creative process as a series of distinct stages:

- The first stage is one of *preparation*, where you collect the data and resources needed to begin to study a problem.
- The second stage is *incubation*, where you can dwell on various ideas and feelings without an intense (or even conscious) effort at a solution.
- Third comes the stage of *illumination*, or what has been called the *Ah-ha!* phenomenon, during which you have a solution or insight spring suddenly into mind.
- The final stage is *verification*, during which you analyze the details of your insight, and conduct any necessary experiments in order to gather additional data.

This process certainly looks familiar to anyone who has tried to come up with an original paper, idea, work of art, or experiment. Your challenge as a teacher is to develop ways to incorporate these processes into your instruction. Your primary job is to give students the information and support they need to become more aware of what will enhance their own creative potential.

Organizations and Innovation

Serious research into the role of creativity and innovation has occurred to a great degree in the business community; but the results of their investigations are clearly applicable to higher education as well. In their best-selling book, *In Search of Excellence*, Peters and Waterman (1982) conclude that creativity is one of several core qualities common to the best American companies. In a follow-up book, *A Passion for Excellence*, Peters and Austin (1985) distill these two qualities that theoretically ensure excellence in one's profession, a passion for quality and a passion for innovation. In each successful company they studied, employee risk-taking was actively encouraged. In addition, employees were given time to create away from the stresses of daily production. Working arrangements were designed to maximize human contacts, with dividers replacing walls, for instance. One example they give is that of a Hewlett-Packard plant, in which there is a feeling of open, informal, and ongoing interaction; this atmosphere is produced by design, and, the authors argue, is intimately tied to the health of the company.

Postsecondary instruction will need to change in much the same way, if creativity is indeed to be a driving force. Teachers should de-emphasize passive learning, drill and practice to make room for exercises that are relevant to students' interests, and which promote active learning within a social context. If you can encourage this kind of climate, student participation should become less standardized and more personalized. Unusual or novel responses to problems will become common. In turn, students will feel a greater sense of personal validation if they are less constrained by a rigid adherence to correctness or some predetermined structure, while for you, teaching will become much more interesting. In addition, letting your own personal interest and energy flourish, and tapping into student interest, should help keep everyone more energized and engaged.

A Whack and a Kick

In his popular books on creativity, Roger von Oech describes the creative process and how each of us can increase our own inventiveness. In *A Whack on the Side of the Head*, von Oech (1983) discusses the "locks" that confine our minds:

- The insistence on the "right" answer
- A preoccupation with what is assumed to be logical
- A conforming impulse to follow the rules
- The call for practicality
- The pressures to stay on task
- The avoidance of ambiguity
- The fear of making mistakes
- The prohibitions against play
- The commandment to be serious
- The assumption by many that they lack creativity

Opening these locks, insists von Oech, is something we all can and should do, and higher education is a great place to contribute to this process. As an academic, you really do have a cultural license to "whack" and "unlock"; perhaps even a professional responsibility. You are in a good position to encourage risk-taking and innovation; you can challenge your students to extend themselves beyond their self-imposed limitations. Resist the urge to spend all your energies filling their heads with details: instead, challenge students to embrace the complexity of an issue, and to confront the big questions, to offer hypotheses, and dream about possibilities. You can nurture a climate which supports creativity, and thereby tap a source of energy and enthusiasm from which everyone can draw.

von Oech offers yet another fun and useful insight into the creative process in a companion book, *A Kick in the Seat of the Pants* (1986). Here he identifies four roles which a creative person plays — explorer, artist, judge, and warrior. By taking on these roles in class, you can provide a model for the creative process at work, and use the process to create more innovative approaches to teaching and learning. While von Oech has worked extensively with businesses that wish to cultivate creativity, his ideas are readily applicable to education. Indeed, higher education may well warrant a more serious attention to creativity than the business community.

Limited by local traditions and isolated from other professionals in class (Sarason 1982), teachers at all levels could benefit by learning more about innovation. As an *explorer* in class, you can venture more into uncharted waters, exploring what exists in fields other than your own. Each semester, you could consider a relevant new topic or book. As an explorer, and as a teacher of explorers, you can show your students how to break out of mental ruts, to analyze and overcome a natural reluctance when encountering new material.

As your exploration progresses, you can play the *artist* and show how intuitive impressions and non-rational leaps can be exploited to deepen understanding. As an artist, you can give yourself permission to break more rules, to fool around, and let your thinking roam and ramble as you pursue fresh insights. Students may need your help here, especially new students. Many are looking primarily for correct answers, and for what you will test. This is especially true for those younger students who are operating on the lowest level of development as identified by Perry (1981, 76-116). Accordingly, some will feel intimidated by an academic environment which values independent, free-wheeling thought. You may have to demand that students extend themselves, and assure them that this kind of unfettered thought is a powerful engine for their own continuing intellectual development.

Once you make use of your artist capabilities, you can regroup and take on the role of *judge*, using your critical eye to assess new ideas and decide on those which seem more promising. In class, you can lead a discussion about what works, what does not, and why. Look for strengths and flaws. Here, you confront von Oech's fourth role, the *warrior*, where you and your students can take action and put your best ideas into practice. For example, students can work individually or in groups on any number of projects or presentations. Field work also allows them to put ideas into practice and try out new skills.

Synectics

William J.J. Gordon (1961) has also researched applications of creativity in business and industry. He coined the word *synectics* which is made up from the Greek roots *syn* (to bring together) and *ectics* (diverse elements). Gordon described his basic assumptions about creativity in ways that have implications for teaching on campus as well:

- Creativity should not be considered mysterious.
- Creativity can be developed and used productively in all fields.
- People can be trained to be more creative.

Gordon also points toward the value of the *nonrational* in fueling creativity. Because of what each of us has experienced, what we have been told and what we have read, our language, the boundaries of our memories, and our world views are well established. Encouraging creativity may require you to quiet your thinking and open up more to your feelings, your intuition, and your imagination. Accordingly, Gordon recommends that you focus more closely on feelings and concrete experiences as catalysts for fresh perspectives and new insights.

More specifically, Gordon focuses on *metaphorical thinking* as an important source of creativity. As a teacher, there are key questions you could ask, including the following:

> What is something *like* and how does it *feel*? For example, to get a new look at teaching, you could ask yourself how a teacher is like a traffic light? Regulating activities; repeating certain responses; offering warnings — blinking yellow or prohibitions — red lights. How would it feel to be that traffic light? Exhausting; routine; mechanical; pressured; automated; uncared for; resented; appreciated only when a power outage creates vehicular anarchy.

You can do this as a formal exercise. First, you use a *direct analogy* to connect one thing to something or someone else that shares at least one similar property. It is very important that this "something or someone else" be concrete and familiar so that students can easily form an image. You then generate a list. For example: How is a student like a *sponge?*

Next, you create a *personal analogy.* The key question is: How does it feel to be this other thing or person? Another list is generated. That sponge, for example, is flexible, absorbent, porous, but with a limited capacity.

Finally, you make what Gordon terms a *compressed conflict* connect back to the original topic. The key question is: How is this something or someone both (feeling #1) and (feeling #2) at the same time? How is a sponge *absorbent* and *limited* at the same time?

These questions and activities may appear contrived, but they illustrate important aspects of creative thinking. Moreover, taking some time for these types of activities adds variety to the class as well.

You can then repeat the steps described above so that students get to practice thinking creatively. Equipped with a descriptive set of images and feelings, students can return to the original topic with new insights and ideas. These new ideas can help students look at old topics with a fresh perspective (*making the familiar strange*) or better understand new or difficult concepts with the help of common references (*making the strange familiar*).

Many teachers find these kinds of activities useful in getting students started on writing projects, and in helping them to relax their preconceived biases — which in turn allows them to take a fresh look at the material. This method of jump-starting creative thought can be highly stimulating for students, and encourages them to take risks and step out of their mental routine. Remember: at this point in the process, there are no right or wrong answers, just feelings and impressions. The time for evaluation of the process comes later. Students benefit from this freedom as a change from standard classroom activities (discussions, exams, papers) that usually result in their performance being judged. Everyone here should participate actively — including you. Every time you connect some idea or theory in your course to current events or issues, you help students make the necessary connections between what they know and what they need to learn.

Active Learning

Creative activities require active student involvement, exploration, and experiential learning — approaches all too often neglected when the focus for instruction is fixed on information transmission and content coverage. Developmentalists like Piaget, Bruner, and Perry as well as other critics of traditional approaches like Tobias and Belenky et al., argue that students benefit greatly from these kinds of activities, especially those who get discouraged by the typical lecture format which forces information primarily in one direction. Visual and kinesthetic learners certainly benefit when they can see and touch objects which relate to their studies. Those students in touch with their feelings usually appreciate these kinds of opportunities. Those who prefer a more social context for learning can also benefit.

Discovery Learning

Discovery learning engages students as active participants in the pursuit of knowledge, allowing them to confront a puzzle, a problem, or a challenge, and to follow their own lead towards a solution. As such, discovery learning is dependent upon innovative creativity in the classroom. Instead of listening passively as you describe a problem and its solution, students using a discovery approach pose questions, discuss possibilities, and conduct experiments, which allows them to tap their own energies, experiences, creativity, and resources as they seek a deeper understanding of the subject matter. With its emphasis on active engagement, discovery learning involves students in what Bruner (1966) calls "the process of knowledge-getting."

Joyce and Weil (1996) enumerate the basic premises of this approach, what Suchman (1962) termed "inquiry training":

- Students inquire naturally when they are puzzled.
- They can become more conscious of their own thinking (meta-cognition) and how best to analyze it.
- New strategies can be taught directly and added to existing ones.
- Cooperative inquiry enriches thinking and helps students to learn about the tentative, emergent nature of knowledge and to appreciate alternative explanations.

Both Bruner and Suchman emphasize how students are empowered when they are allowed to approach a problem, formulate a strategy for attacking it, and solve it for themselves.

Discovery Across the Disciplines

A variety of teaching environments lend themselves readily to a discovery approach. In the science laboratory, the art studio, the music practice room, or the theater, students often arrive at their own insights or interpretations as their studies progress. In each of these environments, learning is grounded in tangible materials — be they the chemicals, equipment, and procedures for an experiment, the clay for a sculpture, the brushes for a painting, a musical instrument or score, or the text, props, and set associated with a play. These tangible elements provide a basis for independent student exploration. Any discipline can exploit the benefits of discovery learning: survey your curriculum and select whatever parts would fit into a discovery learning plan.

The principles of discovery learning can be adapted to the lecture hall as well. Open-ended questions, a current problem in the discipline, even a curious sidelight of the subject can focus student attention. By challenging students, by building off their interests and giving them practice in thinking, by helping them learn to evaluate their own positions and those of others, you can help students learn how to discover what is most relevant or meaningful to them.

As an intellectual activity, discovery learning taps both cognitive and affective abilities. It is generally most successful at the beginning of study on a particular subject, when students meet to pool their knowledge and hunches as a way to better comprehend the matter at hand. At this stage of instruction, breaking a large class into small groups allows individual students to draw upon a greater pool of information, to confront a range of ideas, opinions, and possible solutions, to test and compare different answers, and to make inferences based upon multiple perspectives. When the class reassembles as a whole, these groups can then present their results to one another and receive the benefit of additional feedback.

> Marcia Taylor (Theater Arts) regularly incorporates discovery exercises in her studio classes. To overcome the limitations of performances that are purely intellectual inventions and to help students make their acting more natural and believable, Taylor often encourages them to trust themselves to discover what works. In one exercise, actors work in pairs, focusing on a single line of a scene at a time. By varying the tone, pitch, and timing of their delivery, as well as gestures and movements that accompany these lines, students "discover" the combination of possibilities that feels best to them.

A discovery lesson also allows teachers to combine two essential — though often disparate — elements of their professional responsibilities. By designing lessons which incorporate and highlight the uncertainties and quandaries of scholarly research, teachers can find a way to bridge their roles as instructors and scholars. At the same time, they can also give students a glimpse of what scholars face as they explore the frontiers of their profession.

Questions, Empathy, and Encouragement

For a discovery lesson to be successful, the mental and emotional set of the students is of crucial importance: they want to be ready to learn. After choosing a question, problem, for the lesson, you must present it in a way that piques student curiosity and provokes their thoughtful consideration. From that moment on, you should also be prepared for some degree of unpredictability. The process that evolves demands that you be sensitive to student frustrations and anxieties; you should also resist the urge to give answers too quickly, or to rescue students when they struggle. Some hints and a lot of encouragement may be your best responses as students grapple with the unknown, raise questions, frame hypotheses, and test their ideas.

When using a discovery approach, your primary goal is to design challenges which will engage students actively in exploration (solutions, possibilities, explanations), and thereby stimulate thinking and rethinking of a problem.

Although your questions may generate some tension, they can also serve as a catalyst for growth. If you only ask questions which you are fully prepared to answer, however, student participation may drop dramatically.

Rowe (1974, 81-94) also stresses the importance of "wait time" after you ask a question. Because teachers frequently underestimate the time required for students to think about questions and formulate their own responses, Lowman (1995) suggests counting slowly and silently to ten while calmly scanning the room. If there is still no response, you can move to another part of the room and then rephrase the question in shortened version. Once the class is familiar with you and with this approach, such long waits are rarely necessary.

Assessment

When students are challenged to discover principles or concepts on their own, there are no easily quantifiable ways to evaluate learning. In such cases, you must rely more upon your own ability to assess critical thinking as it plays out in class discussions, conversations, assignments, projects, papers, and presentations. Because the goal of a discovery lesson is the thinking process rather than any single correct answer, you can do more to watch students at work: ask open-ended questions, listen carefully to explanations, reflect back insights, and generally do what you can to facilitate student self-instruction.

Discovery assignments can challenge teachers to broaden their expectations of student capabilities and needs. Often those students you consider to be among the "best" in class — those who complete assignments on time, who come to class prepared, participate actively in class discussions and score well on traditional assessments of learning — may struggle when called upon to analyze a problem critically and independently. Conversely, students who are often disengaged may come to life when you challenge them with a discovery lesson. Throughout the process, cooperative groups can prove valuable for students who experience difficulty or need the support of others to take risks. As students work together, the collective effort to achieve understanding benefits everyone.

Although confusion, noise, and occasional frustration may occur, the exploration of a discovery lesson can be lively, interesting, and fun for both you and your students. If you are the type of teacher who needs to be in control at all times, you may have problems initially accepting the unpredictability of this approach. By experimenting, however, you are modeling the same qualities you want your students to adopt.

In my own educational psychology course, I love to model discovery lessons for future teachers. When dealing with Piaget's notions of cognitive development, for instance, I like my students first to watch a videotape of first graders undergoing various assessments. Children who have not yet developed the ability to "conserve" will typically insist that a ball of clay rolled out into a cylinder has more clay because it looks like it does! These same children will watch when the same amount of water is poured into glass containers of different sizes and insist that "there is more in the taller container." How could that be? I ask. What's going on? Quickly, my students realize how visual cues are dominating the thinking of these students and preventing a "more logical conclusion." Seeing these children perform on the videotape helps my students discover the real meaning of what was written in the text, material heretofore only memorized for exam purposes but rarely understood. The keys here are that the insights flow from the students themselves. I pose the problem or puzzle, ask the questions, and try to guide the discussion toward a new understanding.

Creativity exercises can also promote discovery. For example, I'll often have students write a paragraph about creativity. I then take them through the synectics exercises described by Gordon, and we look at creativity through various manifestations, "what it's like." For example, students may describe creativity as a "hurricane," an "improvised jazz tune" or a "maze," "fireworks," a "rainbow." It's important here to insist on concrete references in which students can see and touch things physical. I then have them generate feeling words associated with each, "how they would feel as these things." Here they offer up words like "powerful" (how it would feel to be a hurricane), "dynamic" (how it would feel to be a jazz tune), "confused" (how it would feel to be a maze), "exploding" (how it would feel to be fireworks), or "dazzling" (how it would feel to be a rainbow).

Remember, all of this is flowing out of the original focus on creativity. From these feeling words, I would then pick apparent opposites to push, pull, and stretch on their ideas. "How is creativity both powerful and dynamic at the same time?" "How is creativity confused and dazzling at the same time?" After some of this, I ask my students to write a new paragraph about creativity, drawing on any of the ideas discussed during the exercise. Now comes the discovery: I ask these students to compare the two paragraphs and explore the differences. Typically, they then come to a new awareness of the restraints they were used to putting on their own thinking, and how the imaging, feeling, and stretching we did put some life and interest into their writing.

It's also great fun. Engaging. Lively, with lots of laughter. Silences, too, as students stretch to come up with metaphors, feelings, and explanations for the seemingly bizarre. A terrific change of pace with some wonderful learnings attached. I always try to spend ten minutes or so debriefing these kinds of activities so that my students are thinking about their own thinking. I often like to ask students to write about these processes in journals and on exams.

Bill Timpson

EXERCISES

1. Think back to something you discovered for yourself. An example from your own research, perhaps. Try to remember as many of the details as possible surrounding the discovery. Where did it take place? How did it happen? How long did it take? What were the conditions you faced? What were your feelings and impulses? With these thoughts in mind, consider the students in your classes. How can you best help them to develop their own abilities to discover?

2. Using a subject that you enjoy and with which you are reasonably familiar, create a discovery lesson. Consider a puzzle, a dilemma, a paradox, a problem — anything that could engage the attention of your students and stimulate them to think. Write out the questions you will ask as you guide students in their discovery.

3. Reflect back to times when you have felt especially creative. What allowed you to create? Who encouraged you? How could you incorporate these factors into a classroom activity or course assignment?

4. Try Gordon's recommendations on yourself. What is your own creativity like? How do each of those descriptions feel? How is your own creativity like any two of those feeling descriptors? Now describe your own creativity having done all that. Do you notice any differences in what you thought before and after these *stretching* exercises?

CORE CONCEPTS

Knowledge as process

Inquiry

Discussion

Readiness to learn

Tension as a catalyst for change in thinking

Wait time

Motivation

Creativity:

- It is not mysterious
- It is similar across disciplines
- It can be developed with practice
- It involves the nonrational (feelings, intuitions, images)
- Its development is like stretching
- It can be enhanced by the use of metaphors and analogies
- It requires certain roles (explorer, artist, judge, and warrior)
- It can be fun, challenging and engaging for students and instructors alike

CHAPTER SEVEN

Group Learning

We are currently leaving an era of competitive and individualistic learning. The 'me' classrooms and 'do your own thing' academic work are fading, and we are entering an era of interdependence and mutuality. The current trend is for 'we' classrooms and 'we are all in this together' learning.

David W. Johnson, Roger T. Johnson, and Karl A. Smith
Cooperative Learning

In the context of an increasingly diverse campus community, cooperative groups are an efficient way to link individual student efforts, allowing them to use their energies and differences to assist and support each other's learning. As the teacher you also get to interact with students on a smaller, more personal scale. By grouping individuals with different abilities, backgrounds, and viewpoints, you can accomplish much more than content coverage. When managed effectively, groups provide a social foundation that bolsters students' critical thinking skills and creativity. The lessons learned by cooperating with others in group activities can have value within and beyond classes. (Note that we will use a variety of terms interchangeably. While some may want to argue over the nuances which distinguish *group learning* from *cooperative* or *collaborative* learning, we will not. The underlying principles are identical, and there seems to be no need to confuse readers who simply want to know what works.)

Learning groups represent a powerful alternative (as well as a supplement) to the traditional lecture format. By augmenting large class meetings with small group activities, teachers can share some of the responsibility for

James Treat (American Studies) employs small groups to facilitate cooperative learning experiences that reflect the tribal values at the heart of his courses in Native American studies. Sociologist Pamela Roby uses two-person listening/learning sessions as part of her course on the sociology of learning. Seven different times during the quarter, pairs of students in her course meet together for two hours to discuss the readings, examine their own experiences with learning and achievement, and undertake related activities. To provide guidance for students during out-of-class sessions, Roby authored a listening/learning guide, which she continuously revises on the basis of students' experiences and suggestions.

instruction with students. Students become more active in this context; gone is the passivity associated with listening and note-taking. Writing instructors, for example, can easily use small groups to provide prompt and varied feedback on writing assignments: the benefit to students can be immense — since the response to an essay from a teacher who is reading sixty other essays at the same time will be frequently (and understandably) tardy and brief. In this way, students and their groups can be an indispensable part of the instructional process.

Active Learning

Cooperative groups ensure that students engage actively with course material, necessitating participation in ways which are not possible otherwise. Learning can become more personalized in a group, as students interact with their classmates over ideas in meaningful and intellectually stimulating ways in such an environment, students are better able to make connections to other parts of their knowledge base, and expand the limits of their thinking in ways that cannot be "lectured into" a student. Previous knowledge, experience, and interest all affect each student's construction of meaning, and these elements must necessarily come from the students themselves.

A learning group is also a place where students can speak about ideas they do not yet fully understand. While they share their thoughts with others, hear the reactions and the reasoning of others, students can become more aware of the depth and breadth of their knowledge. They also can discover what they *don't* know. Unlike the lecture format, where teachers present information in a sequential and orderly manner, group learning can help students zero in on their intellectual blind spots, showing them precisely what part of their thinking is unformed, flawed, or confused. Collaborative projects allow students to deepen their understanding of concepts, and integrate new information into a meaningful, coherent, and defensible system. By such a construction of meaning, students make new information their own.

Cognitive and Affective Outcomes

In *Learning Together and Alone*, David and Roger Johnson (1994) compare cooperative, competitive, and individualized learning models, concluding that cooperative learning in groups is the most effective and efficient approach across a wide range of learning goals: for mastery of concepts and principles, enhanced verbal ability, reasoning, problem solving skills, creative thinking, and general self-awareness. By engaging actively with raw information, or with general concepts and principles, students in groups discover an increased ability to retain, apply, and transfer new knowledge. In addition, they develop democratic values and a greater acceptance and appreciation of individual differences. The Johnsons document studies at all levels and across the disciplines to support these conclusions.

When groups function well, improved interpersonal communication naturally follows. With some guidance on your part, students can use their groups as mini-labs for improving their interpersonal skills, for learning how to listen and express themselves better, how to address conflicts, negotiate compromises, and reach consensus. A learning group also lends cultural diversity, which is a distinct advantage: as students from different backgrounds contribute, the level of discussion expands and deepens. Also, a well-run and highly diverse learning group activity usually results in more comprehensive mastery of material.

> Economist and mathematician Miriam Landesman uses materials developed at the University of California, Berkeley's Lawrence Hall of Science EQUALS program to guide undergraduates through problem solving in cooperative groups. The problems to be solved are divided into four to six parts, each of which is written on a separate piece of paper and distributed to a student in the group. Students combine their pieces of the puzzle in order to find a solution. As they work together, they may read their part aloud to others in the group, but they are not allowed to exchange pieces of paper. In this way, no student can sit passively on the side while others do all the work. If students are shy or reluctant to join in, the initial required contribution is often enough to break the ice so that they feel comfortable participating actively in the shared problem-solving process that follows.

Flexibility of Groups

Learning groups are also appealing because they offer a broad range of possibilities for use. Depending on your goals, group size may vary, although five to seven members seems best for ensuring equitable participation by all. The length of time you devote to any group activity can also vary. You may decide to incorporate a short activity as a change of pace within the context of a lecture, for example, or introduce a collaborative assignment which lasts the entire class period. In large classes where seats are bolted down, you can have students consult with others seated nearby or assign projects to be pursued for the most part outside the classroom. Weekly assignments or term projects can also be organized cooperatively. Because students are often busy, you may have to help students get their groups started: for example, you can schedule a time and place for those who want to form study groups, or use e-mail to link students outside of class.

For some cooperative projects it is possible to divide the labor so that group members take responsibility for learning material or developing skills individually before coming back together to contribute to the whole. This technique, often used by students in study groups to manage their time more efficiently, has been dubbed "the jigsaw" because each participant contributes an essential piece to the completed puzzle. The jigsaw is an excellent way to help students prepare for an upcoming exam. After dividing course material into four parts, ask each member of a group of four to take responsibility for one of the parts. Students leave their original groups and meet together in new groups to compare notes and discuss their assigned parts. When the original groups reassemble, each member has an essential contribution to the group. There is usually high participation, efficient sharing, and genuine group bonding during this kind of structured review period; the mutual interdependence of such a group encourages all students to perform their part well. Once students experience the benefits of this type of learning, they may be more likely to continue their cooperative studies outside of class. Harnessing these student resources and nurturing their feeling of responsibility toward their peers will help you support and assist student learning in ways which are more far-reaching than you can hope to accomplish by yourself.

The Teacher's Role

Obviously, collaborative learning has its own inherent challenges and complexities. Bouton and Rice (1983, 37-38) point out that the success of individual students in mastering course content is intimately tied to the quality of the interaction taking place among members of the group. Group learning, however, does not entail handing over full responsibility for a class to the students; rather, you temporarily surrender your role as sole expert, and focus instead on designing and managing collaborative learning activities where students can be active in enhancing each other's understanding.

Michaelsen (1983, 14-19) describes the tasks facing teachers who choose to use learning groups. They include:

- Forming the groups
- Building and maintaining group cohesiveness
- Sequencing instructional activities
- Organizing material
- Developing and managing group-oriented classroom activities
- Evaluating performance
- Providing feedback

In this discussion we cannot ignore the importance of your role as manager of the group experience, or the time commitment which this can represent. If you are used to more traditional lecturing, you may need to concentrate on a different set of skills to stimulate effective group work. For example, you will want to monitor groups closely so that workloads are distributed fairly and all students contribute to the communal effort. Some groups may require regular supervision in order to keep on task. You will also have to watch out for "collaborative" misinformation where incorrect "solutions" are passed around unchecked.

As for assessment, most faculty members who use cooperative learning establish special means of measuring both individual and group progress. If you decide to assign a group grade, you can expect a mixed response from students: on one hand, they appreciate the support and assistance they receive from other group members, the mutual interdependence which motivates cooperative learning; on the other hand, some students will be understandably anxious about their dependence on others when their grade is on the line. While this anxiety can

> Mathematician Ken Klopfenstein often begins class in his linear algebra course with twenty minutes of group work. Assigned to prepare a written and oral presentation for the group on a particular problem, students take turns and then give each other feedback. Questions and corrections fly back and forth as students struggle to articulate their developing understanding of mathematics. When stumped, students can find Klopfenstein near at hand; or if he's tied up with another group on the other side of the room, a nearby group may work just as well. When asked about the process, students will usually describe the benefits in two ways: first, they usually learn the material better when they have to prepare it as a presentation for others, asking themselves a variety of questions as they anticipate what their groupmates will want to know; second, they hear solutions explained in new ways that are different from what their text or teacher would have used.

create tensions within groups, it can also promote greater effort and enhance performance, both collectively and individually. In any case, make sure that students feel free to approach you with any concerns or worries they may have in this regard.

When the time comes to evaluate a project, it is a good idea to require group members to evaluate their own performance as well. After assuring students that the information they provide will be kept confidential, ask them to identify positive aspects of the group experience, situations that were problematic, and what recommendations they can offer to improve the process in the future. In addition, you might try requiring students to maintain a journal in which they can explore their own reactions to this kind of assignment, thereby developing greater awareness about the group process. All of this information can help you fine-tune your future use of the group-learning format and help nurture student skill in teamwork — an understanding that can be useful in a variety of contexts throughout life.

Impact on Students

Because group assignments provide valuable support and assistance for individual group members, they serve as a kind of instructional infrastructure, empowering students to assume greater responsibility for their own learning. Through the interdependence of the group learning format, students can learn to communicate more effectively with peers, work efficiently with others, define a task, divide up labor, and resolve conflicts. The mutual support students give each other will also encourage a risk-taking attitude that greatly encourages independent achievement.

Well-managed group projects also can contribute to a sense of community and camaraderie, resulting in a general boost in morale for students and teachers. Apathy, absenteeism, and poor performance often decline. In a similar vein, Maimon (1983, 58) recommends collaborative groups as a means to overcome the isolation and loneliness experienced by graduate students, particularly in the humanities. Unlike scientists, who commonly work in groups in the laboratory, other students often spend many solitary hours in the library. At the undergraduate level, however, the situation facing students may be very different. Tobias (1992), for example, notes that many talented students often report feeling discouraged in large introductory science classes, which are frequently information-driven and graded competitively on a curve — both of which tend to be inherently isolating.

Students unfamiliar with the group approach or unskilled in basic communications may face initial difficulty and frustration. Individuals with a strong preference for independent learning, for example, may really struggle within this format. Others will feel frustrated when their inability to explain themselves, understand others, or negotiate differences impinges upon their comprehension of the material. While the Johnsons (1994) encourage the use of heterogeneous groupings so that the diverse abilities needed for success are built into every group, unsuccessful projects can exacerbate these differences. If conflicts do arise among group members, you can help students by actively teaching the requisite social skills needed for effective teamwork. Individuals and groups often need guidance in learning to work together effectively. In this period of great concern for promoting diversity on campus, cooperative experiences can be a very powerful means for enhancing human relations and learning.

Alternating Instructional Strategies

Indeed, learning groups are rapidly taking their place alongside the lecture and the discussion as a popular mode of instruction in higher education. Finkel and Monk (1983, 92-93) point to the varying functions of a teacher and how these can be shared with students. They recommend that you distinguish among three course components: course activities (e.g., teaching, practicing, experiencing, grading); those people responsible for performing these activities (i.e., you, teaching assistants, graders); and places (times, rooms) in the course where these activities occur. Once you have made this analysis, you can then choose among the various options to maximize students' learning. For example, when can students give feedback to each other and augment what you can provide? When can you ask them to present? As you experiment with instructional strategies, Finkel and Monk recommend that, you and your students remain clear about the boundaries separating one from another, since behavior and expectations vary within each format.

In my own classes, I think I have tried every possible option for group learning, yet I'm still eager for new ideas. Cooperative activities have been that effective for me in promoting learning and a supportive class climate. I have made a real paradigm shift here where I now see students as invaluable resources for instruction and learning, able to provide each other with creative alternative perspectives, feedback, and assistance far beyond what I could ever hope to give as one individual. Of course, I still must manage the process with some foresight, care, and attention.

For example, I commonly require a group project where students, both undergraduate and graduate, must work together to plan, develop, rehearse, facilitate, and then evaluate a learning experience for their classmates. A group grade can help weld individual students into a functioning team. While I find that I must provide some active guidance for these groups as their planning unfolds, giving over some class time to the process, I am invariably rewarded — and my classes enriched — as students interject a wonderful blend of energy, variety, and creativity with these presentations.

At other times, I have had students at both levels cooperate in completing an exam question. While individual contributions are difficult to tease apart, the intensity and depth of the interactions can make this a very viable learning option. I do track individual performance along the way, but the group grade helps promote positive interdependence. In the debriefing process that I hold, I will discuss with students what happened, the perceived advantages and problems of groupwork, how different people responded to it, and what they could do differently the next time. I like to think that I am contributing to their developing vital skills for beyond the course — lifelong benefits.

I have also organized cooperative in-class study sessions, where I will subdivide a class and have certain students work together to master particular content. I then reorganize the class into other groups in such a way that all the material will be covered. In this way, each student becomes an expert and vital to his or her group's overall success. One important advantage to this approach is the potential extension where students carry this benefit outside of class and initiate their own study groups. Light (1992), for example, has reported remarkable benefits, especially in demanding science classes, for students who find others to study with outside of class. Using cooperative study groups in class helps many students who might otherwise go it alone take those vital first steps.

When I ask students to evaluate a course at the end of a semester, the various group activities usually receive top marks. Because these groups become so integral to learning, both in and out of class, students are indeed empowered, active in constructing meaning for themselves and their classmates.

Bill Timpson

EXERCISES

1. Think back to an occasion when you personally experienced the power of group collaboration. What was the make-up of the group? Who played the role of manager or facilitator? For what project had you come together? How did the group interaction affect your own point of view? Was the process harmonious? Was it worthwhile?

2. Choose a major concept or principle that you present to students in one of your courses and design a group project to teach it. Specify your instructional goals. How can you achieve those goals using a group rather than an individualized approach?

3. Now focus on the size and make-up of the learning groups. What do you consider the ideal composition of the groups? What steps will you take to achieve this?

4. Assume that your students have not worked in groups before. What can you do to ensure that the groups function effectively? How can you build cohesiveness among individual members? How will you handle conflicts that arise?

5. Consider the sequence of activities. In the traditional model, lecture and individual study are followed by application and exam. Will you follow this order with your groups? Or will you develop a different sequence of activities to meet your instructional goals?

6. How will you design your group project so that students feel their individual contributions have been evaluated fairly? What means of evaluation will you use? When will evaluation occur in the sequence of activities?

7. Imagine that you are teaching a class of 30 in a classroom with individual student desks. What arrangement of furniture will facilitate group learning? Now imagine that you are teaching a class of 150 in a large lecture hall where all the seats are bolted down. What can you do to utilize learning groups in this discussion setting?

CORE CONCEPTS

Cooperation/collaboration

Shared responsibility for learning

Instructor as observer

Instructor as designer

Instructor as group manager and facilitator

Student engagement

Student empowerment

Student responsibility

Critical thinking skills

Improved social skills

CHAPTER EIGHT

Mastery Learning

Mastery learning means essentially that if the proper conditions can be provided, perhaps ninety to ninety-five percent of the students can actually master most objectives to the degree now only reached by 'good students.'

Robert Gagné, Leslie Briggs, and Walter Wages
Principles of Instructional Design

Mastery learning is an instructional strategy promoted by Benjamin Bloom (1973) and others, designed to maximize success in settings where students come to class with a range of abilities and academic needs. Based on the principle that students should demonstrate competence at one stage before moving on to the next, mastery learning draws on a teacher's assumption that nearly all students can learn, *if* there is sufficient time, adequate materials, and appropriate instruction. When instruction is organized in this way, consistent success can build a foundation of student confidence and enthusiasm that in turn spurs further learning. While much of Bloom's original work focused on students in inner city schools, the concepts that emerge from his work are applicable wherever students come into courses with varying degrees of knowledge, skill, general aptitude, and motivation.

A Challenge to Conventional Instruction

Mastery learning challenges the logic of the bell curve, which assigns grades on a comparative basis, and where a student's success in assessed in reference to the performance of others, instead of being set against a

Psychologist Mary Susan Weldon uses elements of the mastery model when teaching basic concepts in her research methods class. After presenting a concept, for instance, she gives one or more examples to provide a meaningful and concrete context for it. She commonly extends this further by presenting the results of a research study detailing actual experimental design and findings. Throughout this process, Weldon both asks and responds to questions from students, listening to detect confusion and repeating explanations as necessary. All in all, this spiraling of focus around key concepts seems to help reinforce student understanding and mastery.

normative standard. However common bell curve grading may be, this approach to grading has failure built into its very structure. Furthermore, when the rate and mode of instruction are fixed and do not respond to individual needs, student success may depend more on prior preparation (i.e., the quality of a student's high school education) and self-confidence. Many talented students can get lost, defeated, or discouraged when they discover they are in a course that doesn't respond to their needs.

The great benefit of mastery learning lies in the supposition that teachers need no longer be satisfied with poor performance. When teachers take into account differing rates and modes of learning, and alter their course accordingly, the chances for student success invariably improve. In the mastery learning model, teachers ask themselves and their students why some succeed while others fail, and then alter their teaching accordingly. They are then able to explore alternatives and make changes intended to bring up those students who are having difficulty before moving on.

With its emphasis on outcomes, remediation, enrichment, and student success, mastery learning is a significant challenge for teachers in higher education. Furthermore, because it may necessitate a search for new materials, additional time, and alternative approaches, many instructors dismiss mastery learning as an impracticality. There are aspects of this approach worth considering from both a conceptual and a pragmatic perspective, however. When students with special needs, for example, struggle in a conventional class structure, the principles of mastery learning can help their teachers reconceptualize instruction and provide better accommodation. In a math or foreign language course, where new learning builds sequentially upon old, instructors can incorporate elements of mastery learning to ensure adequate preparation of students as they progress from unit to unit.

One notable example of mastery learning is the Keller plan (1968, 69-89), where a university course was redesigned as a self-paced, individualized sequence of curriculum units. The required introductory mathematics course at Colorado State University is also modularized with small tutorials and frequent machine-scored testing replacing the traditional semester-long course structure.

Mastery and Training

The basic principle behind mastery learning is that of *training*, perhaps the oldest of teaching models. In simplest terms, training is the process whereby teachers break a skill into its component elements, and then students learn to perform these elements through observation, approximation, feedback, and practice. The teacher sequences instruction in small enough steps so that feedback can be provided quickly and corrective action taken when necessary. The goal of the training paradigm is observable, measurable learning that students can later transfer to new situations. As in the mastery learning model, instructors must design and provide remedial work until the training is successful.

Training figures extensively in some parts of the academy — the laboratory, the studio, and in individual homework assignments — but its applicability may be overlooked in a class where primary emphasis is placed upon content coverage and the acquisition of knowledge. In many ways, assuming that the traditional lecture format is sufficient to the needs of students is analogous to assuming that you can teach someone how to shoot baskets by explaining to them the physical principles of ballistic trajectory and the anatomy of the human arm. As absurd as this sounds, consider how many academics expect students to master new material merely by listening to lectures.

Focusing on Student Success

Central to Bloom's research are a series of simple, fundamental questions:

- Who is responsible for learning?
- Is it enough that teachers simply cover course material?
- When some students fail in spite of seemingly effective presentations, whose fault is it?
- What is the proper measure of student success?

In carrying out his research on mastery learning, Bloom saw clearly that many students are caught in a downward spiral of failure and damaged self-image because their teachers limit their responsibilities to coverage.

By challenging instructors to assume more responsibility for student learning and by promoting the notion that virtually all students can experience success under the right conditions, Bloom hoped to push education in a new, more positive direction.

In Bloom's view, teachers must redefine their relationships with students and manage instruction so that students receive "doses" of success on a regular basis. Instead of being gatekeepers who attempt to weed out those whose grades are at the lower end of the curve, teachers using the mastery learning paradigm set clear standards of achievement and offer repeated opportunities for students to learn course material before moving on. These teachers must respond to students as individuals, addressing their particular needs and preferences, and providing frequent feedback about their progress toward course goals. As a consequence, the mastery learning approach necessitates that you occasionally reteach certain material if it proves difficult for students, and employ varying approaches when necessary. The cumulative successes that these students then experience can bolster self-confidence, class interest, and motivation.

Bloom calls for a basic change in classroom emphasis: from teaching to learning, from curriculum coverage to curriculum mastery, from a grading system that is competitive to one that is individualized and criterion-based. In this context you become a facilitator of learning, not just the conveyer of information. Such a shift requires you to develop and sustain a core faith in student ability to learn, a factor regularly cited in the research literature as critical for instructional effectiveness (e.g., Berman and McLaughlin 1975; Mackensie 1983; McLaughlin 1990).

Implementation of Mastery Learning

Bloom's approach to instruction includes several key strategies — diagnosis of readiness, task analysis, establishment of criteria for mastery, evaluation of learning, and attention to remediation and enrichment. A brief description of each element follows:

Diagnosis of Readiness to Learn

John Carroll (1963, 723-733) identifies five elements that contribute to a student's academic performance:

1. *Aptitude* or general ability to learn
2. *Ability* to understand instruction, based on what the student already knows

3. *Perseverance*, or personal motivation
4. *Opportunity*, or the time allowed to learn a lesson
5. *Quality* of instruction

The information you gather about the first four of these elements will enable you to enhance the fifth. Assessment tests, quizzes, oral responses to questions, assignments, and careful observations all provide important insights as you diagnose individual readiness to learn. Individualized prescriptions for learning are based upon these diagnoses.

Task Analysis

In order to teach material in such a way as to ensure mastery, you should first determine what you want students to learn, and then break that knowledge down into basic elements. Essential to this step is a clear articulation of behavioral or learning objectives, specifying what students should be able to do to exhibit mastery. These objectives should be stated in concrete terms, using clear verbs such as *solve, state, explain, list,* or *describe.* After specifying these objectives, you then group material to be learned into meaningful segments and then larger sequences so that each objective builds upon those which preceded it. The steps in any sequence, however, need to be small enough that you can provide remediation or corrective measures in an efficient and timely manner.

In my own classes I frequently require students to give one another feedback on their term papers or take-home essay exam questions. I have them turn in one or more drafts with written comments from classmates along with their final drafts. This format allows for peer feedback and practice, two elements important for mastery, but at no cost to my own time and energy. As students assist and learn from each other, there is greater likelihood of success. If any complain that the feedback is not useful, I challenge them to identify what feedback would be most helpful and then find people who can provide it. When I have polled students at the end of the semester about this process, most felt it was valuable. Having students ask for feedback from each other also provides a social framework for mastery learning, often appreciated by students in what could otherwise be primarily individualized and isolated work.

Bill Timpson

Criteria for Mastery

Having determined these learning objectives for your students, you should next decide what constitutes mastery for each objective. Criteria for mastery will vary according to the context, the capabilities of the student, and your own expectations. In mathematics, where much of the curriculum is sequential and hierarchical and where mastery of earlier learning is considered essential for later understanding, teachers typically establish relatively high standards or criteria (80-90% correct on assignments and exams). In the social sciences, where the content is more diverse and less sequential, somewhat lower standards might be acceptable (70-80% correct). In areas where safety is a concern, such as laboratories, much more exacting standards may be needed. Where students are poorly motivated, where they have suffered from multiple experiences of failure, more generous criteria with ample opportunities for remediation may be needed to provide the needed dose of success.

Evaluation of Learning

Questions, assignments, papers, quizzes, labs, and exams all provide ongoing, formative data by which you can assess progress and guide the content and pace of subsequent instruction. By furnishing results as regular feedback, you also help students monitor their own progress. Within mastery learning, grading should be criterion-based, indicating whether or not the stated criteria have been met in each case, rather than norm-based, or dependent upon a student's standing relative to others in the class.

Remediation and Enrichment

For students who fail to meet the established criteria for mastery, you can create remedial lessons and assignments. In essence, you continue to present material until nearly all students demonstrate mastery. In the meantime, those who are ready to move ahead can receive enrichment activities, for instance, assignments which could challenge them to provide alternative explanations and examples of concepts they have already mastered. The goal is to broaden or deepen their knowledge base while slower students continue to work to master basic material.

Impossible! you may be thinking. *Another educational theory gone berserk!* If you currently find that it's all you can do to get ready for the classes you now have, you may be wondering where you would find the resources, the time, and the help to do all this extra work. Before you rush to put this chapter away, however, read on. There are a number of ways to lessen the workload of a mastery learning plan. Consider the application of small cooperative groups, for example. Group learning and peer tutoring are practical and valuable approaches for both remedial and enrichment efforts: while slower students get immediate assistance, faster students deepen their own understanding through teaching, responding to questions, offering alternative explanations and examples, and the like. Computer programs also provide drill and practice opportunities, and since computers possess that wonderful technological quality of infinite patience, they are an excellent resource for individualized learning when either remedial or supplemental work is called for.

Another aspect of mastery teaching extends into the evaluation process itself. Consider allowing students in your classes to critique returned exams and to make a case for grade reconsideration. If students argue, for example, that a particular question was vague or misleading, or that the lecture material differed from the information in the text, make it their responsibility to persuade you and to document relevant sources to support their claims. Because this approach encourages review of the material covered by the exam, it provides both remediation and enrichment as students revisit old material and critique course assessment at the same time.

Flow Charts

Flow charts listing the steps to be taken and the behaviors to be mastered can help you track student performance. At a number of points in the diagram, you can insert checks so that students who do not demonstrate sufficient mastery are recycled through earlier steps before they are permitted to go on to new elements in the chain. A flow chart included in the syllabus or posted in the classroom can serve as a guide for you and your students.

For instance, the communication goals in a course on diversity may include the development of listening skills, empathetic forms of expression, negotiating ability, consensus seeking, and problem solving. Course requirements may include a student presentation, required readings, assignments for practice both in and out of class, as well as follow-up discussions. These objectives can become part of a flow chart, along with more traditional methods of helping students give and get feedback and practice new skills. Such an attention to detail will require extra time on your part, but the skills that emerge could promote high-quality independent and group learning, something beyond the scope of most traditional lecture courses. When students themselves master these kinds of skills, they can then participate actively in promoting their development in others.

Reservations About Mastery Learning

Whereas both Carroll and Bloom point to time as an essential factor in the learning equation, critics of mastery learning ask where that time will come from, especially in large, introductory classes. Those who want to use this approach must understand that there is typically some trade-off between the amount of material covered and the degree to which students are able to achieve and demonstrate mastery. The time you devote to review with a few students could be spent, for example, presenting new material to the class as a whole. Slavin (1991, 295) describes a 1983 experiment by Arlin and Webster, who taught students a unit on sailing four chapters long:

> Students in a mastery learning condition received corrective instruction if they missed more than one item on chapter tests, while students in the traditionally taught condition were allowed to go on. Although mastery students scored much better than nonmastery students on a final test, it took them twice as long to complete the unit.

In addition to reservations about the time required for mastery learning, some instructors simply find the approach too structured. They contend that the required organization limits their creativity, overtaxes their ability to respond to students' needs or classroom conditions, and overburdens them with paperwork as they attempt to maintain individualized records. As for students, some complain that the pace of instruction becomes sluggish while they wait for those who require additional time, effort, and attention. In general, balancing these trade-offs is your job. On the one hand, you must respect your obligation to your fast learners. On the other hand, you must remember the plight of students who do poorly each semester, but may have the talent if the conditions for their learning were optimized. Between these two poles, you will find the optimal course for your resources and abilities.

EXERCISES

1. Consider a skill you have learned, one that required a great deal of coaching and practice. A competitive sport, a foreign language, photography, or gourmet cooking all require careful analysis of component skills, practice with feedback, and success along the way. Think through your own experiences while learning that skill. Could aspects of mastery learning have helped you? Where can you apply the principles of mastery learning in your own teaching?

2. Take your notes from teaching a recent class. Look for opportunities to break down complex concepts or issues into smaller units. What could you have asked or done to assess how many students were really keeping up with you? What should most of them have grasped before you moved on? How could you have ensured more student success?

CORE CONCEPTS

Learning vs. coverage

Training

Diagnosis of prerequisite skills

Task analysis

Criteria for mastery

Formative evaluation

Feedback to students

Correctives (remediation)

Extensions (enrichment)

Time for mastery

Variable modes of instruction

Appropriate materials

Student success

CHAPTER NINE

Metateaching and the Instructional Map

The concept of metacognition originated with Meichenbaum et al. (1985) as a description of the process whereby students take a mental step back and think about their thinking, and where you as a teacher help them do that, learning how to learn better. The debriefing of a discovery learning activity, for example, could include some attention to the various ways in which students attacked a particular problem, what other strategies might be possible and what they could do differently for the next problem. We want to suggest that *metateaching* (thinking about teaching or instructional awareness while teaching) can serve this function for instructors. To help you here, we also want to offer you a visual guide, an *instructional map*, to help you step back from your teaching and develop an overview of the organizing principles you want to use in creating your class plan, something which can help you keep your focus during class.

By helping you plot the interaction of course content and objectives with whatever activities you have planned, the instructional map represents a visual outline of the intended teaching and learning process. The map is designed to provide both conceptual and visual cues for thinking through individual lessons, or for planning an entire course. It can also serve as a systematic check, while you teach, of what you still want to do during the lesson.

Whenever you approach a teaching assignment, you are faced with a range of choices: you could concentrate on knowledge or on concepts; on theory or on experience; on the cognitive (intellectual) or on the affective (emotional). We have designed the instructional map to help you make decisions along three criteria in particular: along the continua from teacher-directed instruction to student-centered learning; from a product-focus (knowledge, ideas, skills) to a process-focus (critical and creative thinking, understanding group dynamics); and from individual to group-based learning.

Teacher-Directed to Student-Centered

Answer this question: will you maximize learning with a lecture presentation, a class discussion, or some combination of the two? Perhaps it would be best to start a discussion about your students' interests. There are myriad intermediate positions along the continuum from directed to independent learning. Although you can cover a great deal of material efficiently in a lecture, you may miss certain opportunities if you restrict yourself exclusively to that approach. While discussions can promote engagement and participation, they can miss important aspects of the structure and organization of your course material. By considering the answers to a few key questions, you can decide more readily upon the exact blend of activities you want along this continuum. Who should learn what? Are there some students who require more than a lecture presentation, more than a discussion? Who should be active to maximize learning?

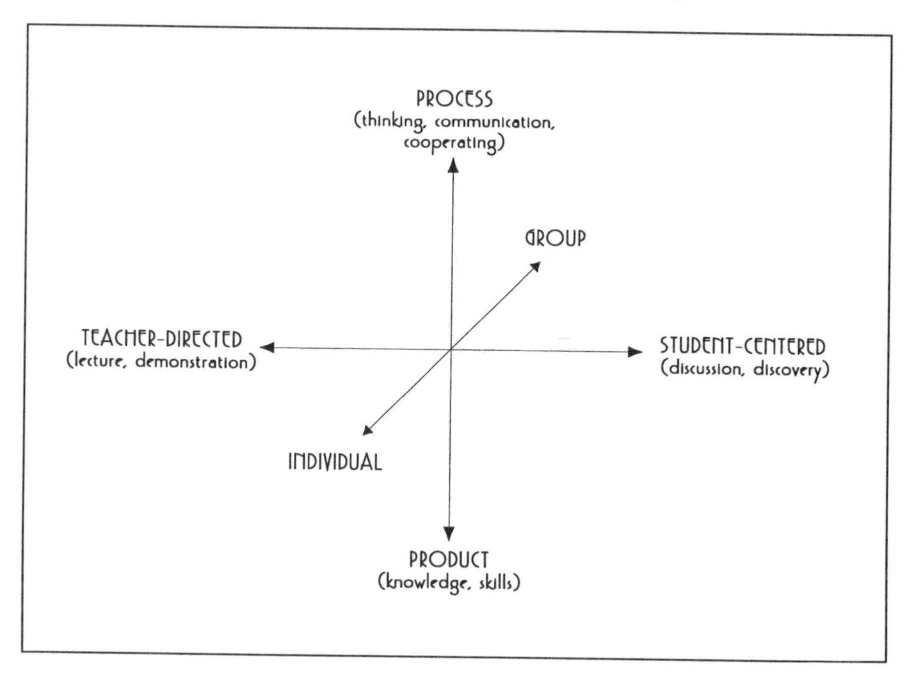

Product to Process

The time and effort you devote to the learning of knowledge or skills can be balanced with whatever you want to dedicate to critical and creative thinking, teamwork, communicating, etc. When you base grades solely on student responses to knowledge-based, objective examinations, for example, you will skew the course emphasis toward product (knowledge and skills). When you require students to write essays, your grading necessarily becomes more subjective and reflective of process skills. Consideration of this continuum can help you develop a better blend of objectives, ranging from the lower levels on Bloom's (1956) hierarchy (knowledge, comprehension, and application) to the higher (analysis, synthesis, and evaluation).

Individual to Group Learning

Individual assignments, both in and out of class, provide for independent practice and assessment. Small group work can provide opportunities for support, assistance, and improved teamwork. While David and Roger Johnson (1994) argue convincingly for the value of group learning activities, individual accountability and whole group instruction will undoubtedly remain important options for teachers in higher education.

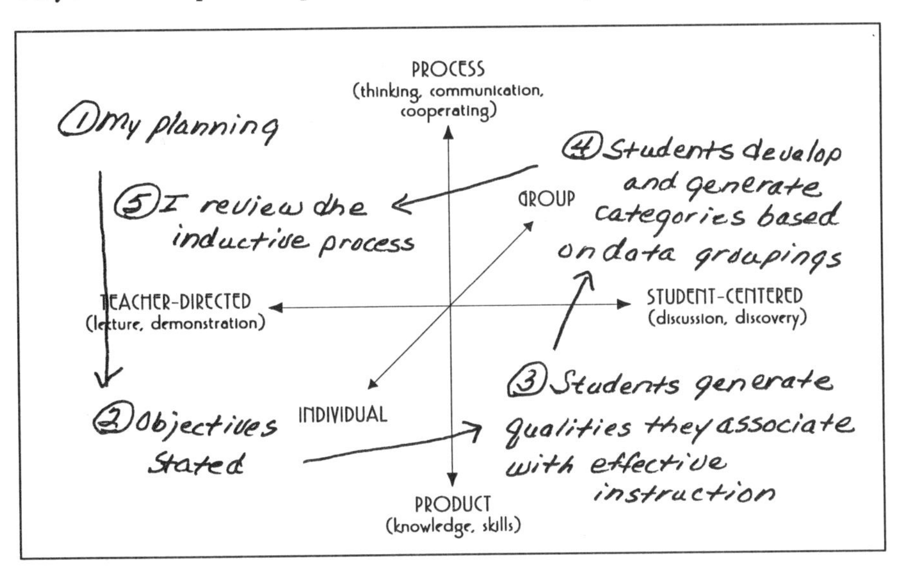

Note: The map above describes an inductive lesson I often use to explore the notion of "effective instruction" where students first generate ideas from their own experience and then compare their conclusions with those I have derived from research. BT

Implementation

The diagrams presented on the previous pages are for use in planning instruction. The horizontal axis displays the continuum from teacher-directed to student-centered instruction. The vertical axis divides product from process. The third-dimensional axis ranges from individual through small- and then large-group instruction. We invite you to experiment with these continua — or any others which better fit what you want to do — noting the impact of various decisions on your teaching, your students, and your courses. By writing in the mix of activities for any given class, you can see the way you want them to combine in meeting your goals and objectives.

I find the instructional map useful as both a visual and conceptual review before class, as well as a mechanism for quick checks during instruction. With respect to the former, the map can serve you much like Ausubel's (1963) advance organizer. Looking at the various options — i.e., teacher-directed or student-centered, process- or product-focused, individual or group learning — reminds me to consider these "delivery" and organizational issues in conjunction with content goals. After reviewing my notes for class and thinking through my goals and objectives, I then sketch out a map and locate the central activities in the order I want. Mapping the process in this way helps me step back from the content — the information and nuances which I often find most interesting, the places where my own research and writing compels my attention — and be able to adequately address course coverage and student learning.

As an example, I offer the completed map (page 31) for a typical lesson in one of my classes. In addition to presenting basic information that I want students to know (product: qualities of effective teachers), I also provide opportunities for them to reflect upon their own experiences (process: describing qualities of their best teachers). Part of the class time is spent in lecture (teacher-directed: presenting a review and overview; describing the research evidence on effective instruction; providing lesson review), and part is reserved for a whole class inductive process (student-centered: data drawn from their experiences are organized, labeled and interrelated). For closure, I then have them think about the process they just completed, and the differences in their own learning when the lecture method is contrasted with this kind of student-centered inductive process. Although students invariably see this kind of participatory process as taking more time, they also recognize that it produces more meaningful and memorable learning.

The variety of activities in this lesson is challenging and fun for me to orchestrate, and highly engaging for students as I help them make collective sense of their own experiences. I really do enjoy the "ah-ha" response I often get at the end, when students see the advantages of this kind of student-centered process. Mapping nurtures my metateaching capabilities as well, helping me to reflect on the teaching-learning process, to think about all those rich and complex interactions where information, ideas, students, text, activities, and I all meet, all those varied combinations and permutations which comprise learning.

Bill Timpson

EXERCISES

1. Reflect back to a recent lecture that you gave or attended. Map out what occurred on the three dimensions (teacher-directed to student-centered; product to process; individual to group). What would have been the impact of shifting the class along one or more of these three continua?

2. Take a topic you will be teaching soon. Consider options at different points of the three continua. Remember that these can shift both within a lesson or across the entire course. How will these impact course goals, objectives, and student learning?

CORE CONCEPTS

Mapping instruction

Instructor-directed to student-centered

Product to process

Individual to group learning

CHAPTER TEN

Peer Feedback and Coaching

The conclusion I am moving toward ... is that teaching skill is not so much taught as it is nurtured into existence. The faculty should know as much as gardeners about necessary nurture and take as much pride in the eventual flowering.

Kenneth Eble
The Craft of Teaching

When put into a context which includes your own expertise, preparation, teaching and skills experience, a solid understanding about the process of learning, and a genuine concern for students, *feedback* may be the single most important mechanism you can tap for nurturing your own ongoing professional development. It is essential that you hear from others about how you are coming across. Are you being heard? Is your material organized well? Is the pace right? Do you show that you care about the material and your students?

Most of us attend to the formal feedback we get from students — the comments at the end of the course as well as the requests we get along the way. Most of us also pay attention to the various other signals which reflect student engagement — tardiness and absences, chatting or reading, sleeping, a general lack of responsiveness to questions, eyes which have glazed over. Some go further and structure activities to solicit feedback from students during the course so that there will be time to make adjustments before the course is over. Some have even seen themselves teach on television, or have invited a colleague or two into class to provide feedback and then offer suggestions about teaching and learning.

While this chapter is about the value of feedback generally, it is more specifically intended to encourage you to explore the use of *peer feedback and coaching*: the practice of instructors helping each other by providing feedback, support, assistance, and ideas while engaging in direct classroom observations and collaborative problem-solving. For those who are willing to solicit feedback this way, we can practically guarantee improvements in teaching effectiveness, increases in learning, and deeper collegial relationships. You will think about your teaching differently. You will get new ideas. You will get to know those who come to observe you in new and different ways; you'll have more to talk about, and more reason to seek each other out, once you've pulled your own teaching out of the closet.

You know your own course material best, as well as your own goals, students, and the physical environments for your classes. When you begin to think about your own teaching and the kinds of feedback you want, you set into motion a very powerful mechanism for self-improvement; i.e., a heightened awareness about your own role in the facilitation of learning coupled with a desire to improve and a knowledge of others who could be helpful in providing feedback and ideas.

> During the fall semester in 1995, I sent myself back to school and sat in three different undergraduate classes — an introductory physics class for non-majors, a mid-level course on linear algebra for math majors, and an upper-division history seminar on American wars in the Pacific. I wanted to see teaching again from the students' perspective and chat with them about learning, and then hold a running conversation with the teachers — all friends and colleagues who were interested in having regular feedback and ideas for improvement. One of the most important contributions I was able to make in each of these classes was to offer my observations and, at times, comments from students about what had happened at various choice points and what other actions (or nonactions) might have been possible. While you can do some things on your own to enhance self-awareness, feedback from someone else may be your most powerful vehicle. I also know I learned a lot from just being the observer.
>
> *Bill Timpson*

Evaluation and Feedback

All too often, however, we think about feedback as evaluation. While school teachers are accustomed to occasional visits from supervisors, instructors in higher education are rarely, if ever, seen by their peers. They are hired primarily for their subject-area expertise, not their teaching ability; the more prestigious degree for working in higher education, the Ph.D., historically represents research competency, not instructional skill or training. Understandably, teachers at the post-secondary level often become anxious about classroom observations; some may even consider visitors as threats to their academic freedom.

Issues of accountability also complicate matters. Although many in higher education accept the practice of assessing research through publications, grants, etc. (where some degree of objectivity can be established through the peer review system), there is much less agreement about the criteria for assessing teaching skill. For this reason, we think it is imperative to shift the focus of faculty development to include feedback, peer support, and assistance — what you as the teacher want. In this way, we can moderate the treacherous waters of assessment and move toward personal initiative and improvement within a positive and collegial climate.

Teachers in higher education also tend to work in relative isolation. Rarely are they in each other's classes, except for the occasional guest lecture. Moreover, academic freedom has often been broadly interpreted as meaning that no one is encouraged to visit or say much about anyone else's teaching, except through interpretation of student evaluations. At universities, the demands of research then only compound this problem, skewing the reward system away from systematic or serious attention to instructional effectiveness and faculty development. Consequently, poor or ineffective teaching practices are allowed to persist on many campuses, with little opportunity to nurture innovation and sustain improvement.

> Bob Richburg is a professor of education who loves to model what he teaches as "best practice." After years of experience in working with new teachers, he has become convinced of the importance of feedback and coaching. Accordingly, he typically demonstrates how this works by putting himself on the line. To model what he recommends, he will surround a sample lesson with a demonstration of feedback and coaching. Before teaching, but in front of his students, he will hold a pre-conference with a colleague/observer, sharing his goals for that lesson as well as the concerns he has and what he would want from the observer. Then the lesson. Then a post-conference where the observer provides feedback and then joins with Bob in a free-flowing discussion of changes that might prove effective. Questions and discussion with students in the class follow. Students love to see this kind of process, where their teacher opens himself to the same kinds of criticism which they routinely get from their instructors. It also gives them a direct experience with something they are expected to use.

In this context, peer feedback and coaching can provide a valuable mechanism for ongoing collegial support, assistance, and sharing — and it's free. By enlisting the support of colleagues, you can create a nonjudgmental climate for your own development as a teacher and learn to benefit from sharing with others your ideas and hopes, efforts and concerns, joys and discouragement. While professional isolation can allow bad habits to persist and inhibit efforts at improvement, a campus community which truly values effective teaching and learning can become closer through a peer feedback and coaching model.

Classroom Complexities

The need for feedback and coaching is growing in higher education. As we have reiterated throughout this book, student diversity and needs are increasing, and with them the difficulties that you as a teacher face. Differences in preparation, motivation, learning styles and preferences put some students at odds with their teachers: can we expect students to make all the adjustments? Issues of gender and race can also add other emotions to the classroom, and you may feel unsure of how best to act and react at various times. Advances in technology regularly create new opportunities and challenges. The observations, support, and ideas which a colleague can offer can be of great help.

The complexities inherent in teaching and learning require you to attend to a whole slew of interactive variables — content, student characteristics, your own values and style, the physical space, and time available — and a feedback partner can help you think through what is happening as well as what other options you may have. For example, you may have specific questions: Are there signs of gender or cultural differences in the ways that students respond, interact, and learn? Who asks what kinds of questions? When are there signs of boredom, restlessness, confusion, or excitement? In general, what seems to work? What doesn't? With the assistance of a colleague, you can discuss these kinds of concerns ahead of time, review the observations after class, reflect on your strengths and weaknesses or where you may have blind spots, and share ideas about possible improvements.

Practices in Other Fields

Peer feedback and coaching occur routinely in many fields. Performers, for example, receive regular and intense feedback. Directors routinely interrupt rehearsals to comment or offer suggestions. This form of coaching is immediate and frequent, and for a good reason: the best possible production. Directors will also give "notes" at the end of rehearsals and performances when everyone can hear and respond, pointing out what works and what doesn't, offering solutions or modeling what they think will work better. Likewise, actors frequently give each other feedback and ideas (Timpson and Tobin 1982; Timpson, Burgoyne, Jones, and Jones 1996). Similarly, athletes receive extensive and intensive feedback and coaching both in practice and competition. Coaches at all levels use videotapes of practices and games to provide additional data for analysis and feedback. Everyone who plays organized and competitive sports accepts these roles, relationships, and processes.

In his groundbreaking work, *The Seasons of a Man's Life*, Levinson (1978) describes the role that mentors play in many fields to help individuals, especially new and junior members of an organization, survive and succeed. As Erikson (1974) reported years earlier, there exists a very natural tendency in middle adulthood, in what he termed the stage of *generativity*, to want to nurture the next generation.

In *Developing Talent in Young People*, Benjamin Bloom and his colleagues (1956) go beyond a description of the place for mentors, teachers, and coaches, detailing how these roles change in the development of world-class talent across a range of different domains — academic (mathematics and physics), artistic (music), and athletic (tennis and swimming). Whereas encouragement and patience are the most common qualities needed when training novices, technical skill becomes increasingly important during the middle years. At the highest levels involving international competition, the best teaching seems to include nearly unachievable expectations for the student, a kind of "master/slave" relationship.

Feedback vs. Evaluation

In our model, peer feedback and coaching offer a system of mutual support and assistance. This is quite different from "personnel assessment" as overseen by administrators. All schools and campuses have some kind of performance evaluation system in place for teachers, and these inevitably create some anxiety. In higher education, teacher evaluations are typically tied to decisions about tenure, promotion, and merit pay. What we recommend here, however, is that feedback and coaching be unhooked from the formal evaluation process, that the focus instead be on feedback, support, and assistance for teachers. In this way, psychological defenses can be lowered, while trust and openness can be heightened.

Coaching Options

Joyce and Showers (1978) have proposed a peer coaching system to provide teachers support and feedback as they work on new skills. Another model for coaching has administrators and instructors "scripting" lessons that they observe, detailing everything that occurs and using various notions about effective instruction as a frame of reference. The approach we propose here uses both perspectives, but places responsibility on teachers to choose their own focus for feedback and coaching. For instance, you may want feedback on a new approach you are trying, or on certain aspects of your lecture. You may want someone to watch particular students who are struggling or offer ideas for energizing a familiar teaching strategy. The focus for coaching is unlimited, and you as the teacher are in the best position to determine what you need and when.

According to Joyce and Showers, at least three distinctly different coaching relationships are possible. In *collegial* coaching, instructors provide each other with support, assistance and feedback. In *technical* coaching, "experts" provide direction and feedback for new skill development. In *challenge* coaching, teachers meet to solve problems. Successful coaching in higher education should include aspects of all three, blended according to each teacher's needs and wishes. This last part is crucial, for it keeps the initiative for growth where it belongs — with you the teacher.

Logistics

While the logistics of peer coaching — who, when, why, where — should be left up to teachers, there must also be administrative support to make coaching work. If leaders in higher education truly value the professional growth for teachers which peer coaching can foster, then they must help provide the necessary support, encouragement, resources, time, and vision. Coaching should not be another "add-on." Instead, it should become a part of regular campus responsibilities.

Essential Factors

There are certain critical factors for the development of an effective coaching relationship.

> *First*, you must be willing to take risks, to rethink old practices, and explore new possibilities, to share ideas and feelings openly, to support colleagues and their needs. While you may feel somewhat cautious during initial observations and discussions, with experience, you can become more confident when experimenting with new ideas.

Second, an essential trust must grow as feedback and coaching progress, allowing you and your peers to interact more easily and candidly.

The *third* element is a positive focus. Our model rests on a very basic assumption that any teacher can improve with study, feedback, experimentation, and practice. During initial observations, those giving feedback may want to concentrate on the positive elements of a lesson first before raising questions or discussing what may have seemed problematic.

Fourth, the focus for the observation should be clear so that observers can collect worthwhile data. Teachers need to request specific comments and data about specific concerns they have. Focusing attention on particular details of your teaching should prove more helpful than getting a general impression of "how the class went."

Because of all the above, the *fifth* requirement for peer feedback and coaching is time, not only because we recommend both pre- and post-conferences in addition to each observation, but because the process is an evolving one which may develop a life of its own and continue over months or years.

The Development of Teachers

The system of coaching and feedback we propose can be tailored to the needs of each individual, at any stage of their career. For new teachers, commonly preoccupied with concerns about self (e.g., "How am I doing?"), it may be most important to provide lots of encouragement, positive feedback, and assurances that the challenges of effective instruction can be mastered in time. As teachers gain confidence and experience, they can focus more on the tasks of teaching, and observers can concentrate more on how well various approaches seem to be working as well as sharing ideas for further consideration. Later, when the mature teacher's focus shifts to students, feedback can expand and refer to any aspect of the teacher-student relationship and the teaching-learning process. Frances Fuller and colleagues at the University of Texas-Austin have published a series of papers describing the effects of feedback and teacher concerns on professional development (e.g., Fuller 1969, 207-226).

Wilsey and Killion (1982) proposed four stages of adult development that we believe have relevance for a peer feedback/coaching system. (Notice the parallels to Perry's (1981) model as described in chapter 3.)

Stage 1: Individuals may have a *right-wrong* orientation to situations. There is then only one way — their way — to view the world. Only when these people sense that what they are doing is not working do they see a need for new knowledge. They'll adapt information which does not fit their current belief systems to fit categories that already exist rather than create new ones. Piaget referred to this process as *assimilation*. This kind of person prefers hierarchical relationships and wants to address practical concerns about specific situations.

Stage 2: Individuals begin to break away from strict rules and beliefs. They tend to ask more questions and are more willing to express their points of view, yet they still have difficulty understanding differing points of view. They show an interest in principles and issues, and often want to develop their own applications or adaptations, but they may also resist control by authority.

Stage 3: People recognize that they have a variety of alternatives and can choose the one which seems to best fit a particular situation. They are able to accommodate contradictory information by balancing or connecting differing ideas.

Stage 4: Individuals are able to synthesize information and create additional categories to accommodate new information. They tend to approach problems and situations in a systematic fashion, which enables them to review alternatives and make effective, timely decisions.

Peer feedback and coaching will generally function best with people at stages three and four, where they have the ability to acknowledge a need or problem as well as some skill for initiating change. However, there is clearly a place for support, assistance, and sharing at any stage. Successful experiences with peer coaching at earlier stages may be a catalyst for you moving to higher stages.

A Model for Peer Feedback and Coaching

Pre-Conference

It can be very helpful for you to get together with your invited observer prior to class. This can provide some welcomed personal contact if you are anxious about teaching with a colleague present. Your discussion can help you clarify what you want from the observer and how to best assess it. In actuality, your heightened awareness about your own goals may do much to sharpen your planning and teaching and help you point toward areas for improvement.

Setting Goals for Feedback

It is essential for you to participate actively in setting goals for feedback about your own teaching. When you leave goals or concerns vague, observers are left with only their own subjective judgments. While these kinds of opinions may have some value, lasting improvements are more likely when you can decide on a primary focus and then articulate the kinds of feedback you want.

For example, many teachers are not fully aware of the kinds of questions that they ask in class, or they neglect to pay close enough attention to student responses — or lack of response. Some instructors will ask questions that end up being purely rhetorical. Like quicksand, and perhaps just as unconsciously, some teachers may rush in to fill the void created when no one leaps to respond, thereby "rescuing" students from the quiet, but possibly stifling student initiative and growth in the process. Other teachers may only call on certain students, those who can be counted on regularly for responses. This approach may limit opportunities for others who are less comfortable making public responses but who would benefit from the expectation and encouragement to do so.

When planning for feedback, you should push yourself to make your goals as objective as possible so that observers will be better able to measure, assess and document what you really want, which areas you want to improve. For instance, knowing which students asked what kinds of questions can be very helpful. Were these questions convergent (focusing on a certain answer) or divergent (open-ended)? How did the rest of the class respond? What happened to student engagement or involvement during this time? What happened to note-taking? If you are unsure about what to ask for, ask your observer to listen carefully, reflecting back what is heard. This can help you clarify your own goals.

Recording Data

Having discussed their role with teachers before going into any class, observers should then discipline themselves to record what is requested. The more they can quantify these observations, the better this kind of feedback should be. It is also important for the observer to look for whatever you consider important even if that may seem difficult or impossible to quantify. For example, if you want to do more to challenge students to rethink their assumptions, observers can describe whatever seems relevant, from classroom interactions to facial expressions, silences, and the like. It is important for the observer to stay focused on what you as the teacher want and use whatever data emerges to promote reflection and offer new possibilities.

Providing Feedback in a Post-Conference

You and your observer should then agree to meet some time after class to discuss these observations, share relevant experiences and explore other ideas. Observers should discipline themselves to provide descriptive information on what you requested and refrain from judgment. Judgments are subjective, personal to the observer, shifting the emphasis from your own thoughts and feelings, and leaving you passive, even anxious or defensive. Lasting improvements are more likely to result from your active responses to the data you receive. Providing quantitative and descriptive feedback should evoke less resistance from you and stimulate more open and honest reactions.

Sharing Experiences and Ideas

If asked to contribute, observers can avoid judgment by sharing personal experiences that seem relevant. For example, if pressed for advice, observers can still avoid statements that begin with "You should have ..." Using a phrase like, "If this were my class, I think I would ..." can feel less judgmental and leave the teacher with the responsibility for deliberation. In essence this amounts to a kind of "client-centered" mode of interaction long advocated by psychologist Carl Rogers (e.g., 1951) as a vehicle for building trust and helping someone develop self-awareness, insight, self-confidence, and responsibility for personal change.

Follow-Up Feedback

Teachers in higher education are usually very busy people. Work schedules often undermine the supposedly reflective life, when even your time for thinking can feel pressured by student demands, assorted deadlines, committee work, and other obligations. In this context, the thought of adding to your stock of obligations may seem crazy; however, there are ways to make the giving and receiving of feedback manageable and productive.

If you desire frequent feedback but lack the time to try the peer coaching model, there are other potentially viable sources to consider. Videotaping your teaching can give you much to think about. Although many people are quite fearful about appearing on television at first, most can derive great benefit once past this initial anxiety. Students can also provide valuable feedback. Try asking for written comments from them, at any time during the semester, about how they feel your course is working for them and what changes they would recommend. Many teachers also find it quite helpful to have someone else come in to administer a formal assessment of student opinions, cataloguing appreciations, concerns, and recommendations.

You can also take some time in class to give and receive feedback directly, face to face. In such a "classroom meeting" (Glasser 1969, 1965), you encourage students to share their feelings and thoughts, both positive and negative, about the class at that point and offer reasonable suggestions for improvements. While this may feel threatening, the results can be very healthy and positive. Assuredly, a few criticisms will sting and require some discussion to clarify; other complaints may only reflect the whining of a few who really want to do as little work as possible. With encouragement and polling, you should be able to solicit responses from the entire class, most of whom will respond in a responsible fashion. Furthermore, we know you will love to hear students express their appreciations for the class publicly. You may then want to negotiate certain suggestions (e.g., study guides for the exams) and experiment with their implementation. Afterwards, the atmosphere should feel more more clear and open. Often, then, everyone will proceed through the rest of the course with greater resolve and esprit.

Summary

If Schon (1983) is right in stating that the hallmarks of a professional are reflection and the growth that accompanies it, then the value of a feedback/coaching system for instructors in higher education is obvious. As one teacher in a study by McLaughlin et al. (1986, 424-425) reported, "You can only learn to be a teacher if you have a supportive, nurturing environment." Or in the words of another, the lack of opportunity for interaction with colleagues makes "teaching seem less like a profession and more like a job."

At the present, teachers in higher education are much too isolated professionally. For professional development to have an impact, you will need opportunities to interact with colleagues on a regular basis, to observe each other's classes and offer ongoing feedback, support, assistance, and ideas. Campus administrators, in turn, should provide the support and leadership needed for this to occur. We cannot continue to perpetuate what has been an essentially Darwinian environment of "sink or swim" for new and experienced teachers alike.

I had my first feedback session with colleague and friend Dennis Cole, and the experience proved rich and rewarding for both of us. I was initially anxious and, although I usually feel comfortable in front of students, I was unused to having a colleague in class. In addition, somewhere deep down inside my less rational psyche lurked a fear that a negative judgment could work against me, somehow, when decisions about promotion or merit pay came up — a fear echoed by colleagues on various campuses. Why take this kind of risk, especially when others didn't? Yet, I was excited about what we would be able to talk about and that a friend would be sharing in what had always been something I did alone. Peer feedback made sense and seemed promising. It also helped that Dennis is easygoing and likable, that we already had a good working relationship and trusted each other. It also helped that he understood and valued this kind of peer coaching and feedback.

Once class began, however, I forgot about Dennis being there and carried on with teaching as usual. When we sat down later to discuss what happened, I must admit that I got a bit anxious again; just what would his judgment be? Once Dennis showed me his notes, however, and began to describe what he had observed, I was able to relax, listen, and think about the implications. After that, we shifted roles and I talked about my own impressions, trying to clarify my own thinking and goals in light of his feedback. Next, we shared other related experiences and then considered a variety of options.

All in all, I found the whole process quite rewarding. By taking this kind of risk, by pulling someone else into my "teaching closet," I think we developed a new level of trust and understanding. We knew more about each other. After that observation and discussion, we checked in with each other fairly often, providing additional follow-up and support.

Bill Timpson

EXERCISES

1. Consider various aspects of your own teaching. What concerns or questions do you have? Where do you want improvement? What feedback would be useful for you? To what extent can it be quantified? How would you like it delivered? By whom? When? Develop a workable plan to solicit feedback and make a commitment to follow through.

2. Reflect back to a time when you received feedback about your performance as an instructor. This may have come from a colleague, a friend, or a student. Analyze the way the feedback was given and how you received it. What would have made the feedback more useful or increased your own receptivity to it?

CORE CONCEPTS

Feedback vs. evaluation

Peer coaching increases trust and collegiality

Peer coaching increases effectiveness and innovation

Pre- and post-conferences between instructor and observer maximize benefits

For the instructor:

- Determination of goals
- Goals cast in measurable terms

For the observer:

- Reflective listening
- Avoiding judgment
- Sharing experiences when asked

References

Ausubel, David Paul. 1963. *The psychology of meaningful verbal learning: An introduction to school learning*. New York: Grune and Stratton.

Axelrod, Joseph. 1973. *The university teacher as artist*. San Francisco: Jossey-Bass.

Belenky, Mary Field, Blyte McVicker Clinchy, Nancy Rule Goldberger, and Jill Mattuck Tarule. 1986. *Women's ways of knowing: The development of self, voice, and mind*. New York: Basic Books.

Berman, Paul and Milbrey W. McLaughlin. 1975. *Federal programs supporting educational Change, Vol. VI: A summary of the findings in review*. Santa Monica, CA: The Rand Corporation.

Bloom, Benjamin S., et al. 1956. Taxonomy of Educational Objectives: The Classification of Educational Goals. In *Handbook I: Cognitive domain*. New York: Longman Green.

Bloom, Benjamin S. 1973. *Every kid can: Learning for mastery*. Washington, D.C.: College University Press.

Bouton, Clark, and Russell Y. Garth. 1983. Students in learning groups: Active learning through conversation. In *Learning in Groups*, edited by Clark Bouton and Russel Y. Garth. San Francisco: Jossey-Bass.

Bouton, Clark and Beryl Rice. 1983. Developing student skills and abilities. In *Learning in Groups*, edited by Clark Bouton and Russel Y. Garth. San Francisco: Jossey-Bass.

Bruner, Jerome. 1966. *Toward a theory of instruction*. Cambridge, MA: Harvard University Press.

Bruner, Jerome, Jacqueline J. Goodnow, and George A. Austin. 1967. *A study of thinking*. New York: Science Editions.

Bybee, Rodger W., and Robert B. Sund. 1982. *Piaget for educators*. Columbus, OH: Merrill Publishing Company.

Capra, Fritjof. 1991. *The Tao of physics*. Boston: Shambhala.

Carroll, John. 1963. A model of school learning. *Teachers College Record*, 64: 723-733.

Christensen, C. Roland. 1982. Introduction. In *The art and craft of teaching*, edited by Margaret Morganroth Gullette. Cambridge, MA: Harvard University Press.

Dreikurs, Rudolf. 1968. *Psychology in the classroom: A manual for teachers*. New York: Harper and Row.

Eble, Kenneth. 1994. *The craft of teaching*. San Francisco: Jossey-Bass.

Edelstein, Wolfgang. 1992. Development as the aim of education revisited. In *Effective and responsible teaching: The new synthesis*, edited by Fritz K. Oser, Andreas Dick, and Jean-Luc Patry. San Francisco: Jossey-Bass.

Ehly, Stewart W., and Larsen, Stephen C. 1980. *Peer tutoring for individualized instruction*. Boston: Allyn and Bacon.

Erikson, Erik H. 1974. *Dimensions of a new identity*. New York: Norton.

Finkel, Donald and G. Stephan Monk. 1983. Teachers and learning groups: Dissolution of the atlas complex. *Learning in Groups*, edited by Clark Bouton and Russel Y. Garth. San Francisco: Jossey-Bass.

Fox, Robert S., Herbert E. Boies, Edward Brainard, Edward Fletcher, James S. Huge, Ceclia Logan Martin, RRichard Schmuck, Thomas A. Shaheen, and William H. Stegeman. 1974. *School climate improvement: A challenge to the school administrator*. Bloomington, IN: Phi Delta Kappa.

Freire, Paulo. 1970. *Pedagogy of the oppressed*. New York: The Seabury Press.

Fullan, Michael with Suzanne Stiegelbauer. 1991. *The new meaning of educational change*. New York: Teachers College Press, Columbia University.

Fuller, Frances. 1969. Concerns of teachers: A developmental conceptualization. *American Educational Reseearch Journal*, 6: 207-226.

Gagné, Robert. 1985. *The conditions of learning and theory of instruction*. 4th ed. New York: Holt, Rinehart, and Winston.

Gagné, Robert, Leslie J. Briggs, and Walter W. Wager, 1988. *Principles of instructional design*. San Francisco: Holt, Rinehart and Winston.

Gilligan, Carol. 1982. *In a different voice: Psychological theory and woman's development*. Cambridge, MA: Harvard University Press.

Gilligan, Carol, Annie G. Rogers, and Deborah L. Tulman, eds. 1991. *Women, girls, and psychotherapy: Reframing resistance.* New York: Harrington Park Press.

Glasser, William. 1969. Schools without failure. New York: Harper & Row.

Glasser, William. 1965. Reality therapy: A new approach to psychiatry. New York: Harper & Rowe.

Gordon, William J.J. 1961. *Synectics: The development of creative capacity*. New York: Harper and Row.

Gronlund, Norman E. 1985. *Stating objectives for classroom instruction*. New York: Macmillan Publishing Company.

Harel, Idit. 1991. *Children designers*. Norwood, NJ: Ablex Publishing Corporation.

hooks, bell. 1988. *Talking back: Thinking feminist, thinking black*. Boston, MA: South End Press.

Hunter, Madeline. 1982. *Mastery teaching*. El Segundo, CA: TIP Publications.

Johnson, David W. and Roger T. Johnson. 1994. *Learning together and alone*. Englewood Cliffs, NJ: Prentice-Hall.

Johnson, David W., Roger T. Johnson, and Karl A. Smith. 1991. *Cooperative learning: Increasing college faculty instructional productivity*. ASHE-ERIC Higher Education Report No. 4. Washington, DC: The George Washington University, School of Education and Human Development.

Joyce, Bruce R. and Marsha Weil. 1996. *Models of teaching*. Englewood Cliffs, NJ: Prentice-Hall, Inc.

Joyce, Bruce R. and Beverly Showers. 1978. The coaching of teaching. *Educational Leadership*, 40: 4-10.

Kasulis, Thomas. 1984. Questioning. *The art and craft of teaching*. Cambridge, MA: Harvard University Press.

Keller, F. 1968. Good-bye teacher. *Journal of Applied Behvioral Analysis*, 1: 69-89.

Kohlberg, Lawrence. 1963. The development of children's orientation toward moral order: Sequence in the development of moral thought. *Vita Humana*, 6: 11-33.

Levinson, Daniel J. 1978. *The seasons of a man's life*. New York: Ballentine.

Lezotte, Lawrence W., Douglas V. Hathaway, Stephan K. Miller, Joseph Passalacqua, and Wilbur B. Brookover. 1980. *School learning climate and school achievement*. Tallahassee, FL: The Site Specific Technical Assistance Center.

Light, Richard J. 1992. *The Harvard assessment seminars*. Cambridge, MA: Harvard University's Graduate School of Education and Kennedy School of Government.

Lowman, Joseph. 1995. *Mastering the techniques of teaching*. San Francisco: Jossey-Bass.

Mackensie, Donald. 1983. Research for school improvement: An appraisal of some recent trends. *Educational Researcher*, 12(4): 5-17.

Maimon, E. 1983. Graduate Education and Cooperative Scholarship. *Learning in Groups*, edited by Clark Bouton and Russel Y. Garth. San Francisco: Jossey-Bass.

McClelland, David. 1985. *Human motivation*. Glenville, IL: Scott Foresman.

McKeachie, Wilbert J. 1990. *Teaching tips: A guidebook for the beginning teacher*. Lexington, MA: DC Heath and Company.

McLaughlin, Milbury W. 1990. The Rand Change Agent Study revisited: Macro perspectives and micro realities. *Educational Researcher*, 19: 11-16.

McLaughlin, Milbury W., R. Scott Pfeifer, Deborah Scanson-Owens, and Sylvia Yee. 1986. Why teachers won't teach. *Phi Delta Kappan*, 67: 420-426.

Meichenbaum, Donald, Susan Burland, Linda Gruson, and Ray Cameron. 1985. Metacognitive assessment. In *The growth of reflection in children*, edited by Steven R. Yussen. Orlando, FL: Academic Press.

Menges, Robert. 1981. Instructional methods. *The modern American college*. San Francisco: Jossey-Bass Publishers.

Michaelsen, Larry K. 1983.Team Learning in Large Classes. *Learning in Groups,* edited by Clark Bouton and Russel Y. Garth. San Francisco: Jossey-Bass.

Miller, George. 1956. The magical number seven, plus or minus two: Some limits on our capacities for processing information. *Psychological Review,* 63: 81-97.

Nash, Laura L. 1984. The rhythms of the semester. *The art and craft of teaching,* edited by Margaret M. Gullette. Cambridge, MA: Harvard University Press.

Patrick, Catherine. 1955. *What is creative thinking*. New York: Philosophica Library.

Perry, William J., Jr. 1981. Cognitive and ethical growth: The making of meaning. In *The Modern American College,* by Arthur Chickering. San Francisco: Jossey-Bass.

Peters, Thomas J. and Robert H. Waterman. 1982. *In search of excellence: Lessons from America's best-run companies.* New York: Harper and Row.

Peters, Thomas J. and Nancy Austin. 1985. *A passion for excellence: The leadership difference.* New York: Random House.

Piaget, Jean. 1952. *The origins of intelligence in children.* Translated by M. Cook. New York: International Universities Press.

Rogers, Carl. 1951. Client-centered therapy: Its current practices, implications, and theory. Boston: Houghton Mifflin.

Rogoff, Barbara. 1990. *Apprenticeship in thinking: Cognitive development in social context.* NY: Oxford University Press.

Rowe, Mary. 1974. Wait time and rewards as instructional variables: Their influence on language, logic and fate control. Part 1: Wait-time. *Journal of Research in Science Teaching*, 11: 81-94.

Sarason, Seymour Bernard. 1982. *The culture of the school and the problem of change.* Boston: Allyn and Bacon.

Schon, Donald A. 1983. *The reflective practitioner: How professionals think in action.* New York: Basic Books.

Segerstrale, Ullica. 1984. The multifaceted role of the section leader. *The art and craft of teaching*. Cambridge, MA: Harvard University Press.

Shaheen, Thomas A., and W. Roberts Pedrick. 1974. *School district climate improvement.* Denver: CFK Limited.

Slavin, Robert. 1991. *Educational psychology*. Englewood Cliffs, NJ: Prentice Hall.

Suchman, Richard J. 1962. The elementary school training program in scientific inquiry. *Report to the U.S. Office of Education, Project Title VII*. Urbana, IL: University of Illinois.

Tharp, Roland and Ronald Gallimore. 1988. *Rousing minds to life: Teaching, learning and schooling in social context*. NY: Cambridge University Press.

Timpson, William M.; Suzanne Burgoyne, Christine Jones, and Waldo Jones. 1996. *Teaching and performing: Ideas for energizing your classes*. Madison, WI: Magna Publications, Inc.

Timpson, William M., and Christine Jones. 1989. The naive expert challenges the gifted child. *The Gifted Child Today*, 12: 22-23.

Timpson, William M. and David N. Tobin. 1982. *Teaching as performing: A guide to energizing your public presentation*. Englewood Cliffs, NJ: Prentice-Hall.

Tobias, Sheila. 1990. *They're not dumb, they're different*. Tucson, AZ: Research Corporation.

Toffler, Alvin. 1980. *The third wave*. New York: William Morrow.

von Oech, Roger. 1983. *A whack on the side of the head: How to unlock your mind for innovation*. New York: Warner.

von Oech, Roger. 1986. *A kick in the seat of the pants: Using your explorer, artist, judge, and warrior to be more creative*. New York: Warner.

Wilkinson, James. 1982. Varieties of teaching. In *The Art and Craft of Teaching*, edited by Margaret M. Gullette. Cambridge, MA: Harvard University Press.

Wilsey, C. and J. Killion. 1982. Making staff development programs work. *Educational Leadership*, 40: 36-43.

Zukav, Gary. 1979. *The Dancing Wu Li Masters*. New York: William Morrow.

Index

A

B

C

D

E

F

G

H

I

J

K

L

M

N

O

P

R

S

T

V

W

Z